Carpentry and Interior Finish

"*Interior Finish*'s 'old style tricks of the trade' will especially intrigue and aid amateur woodwrights; but neo-professionals will want to have a look at it, too, to make sure they haven't missed anything."

—*Midwest Book Review*

"From preparation and insulation to cabinets and bookcases, this guide covers every aspect of interior finish."

—*Woman's Day Kitchens and Baths*

"A must for any beginner, and probably can teach even experienced builders a thing or two."

—*Sacramento (CA) Union*

"Here's a handy, reasonably priced and easy-to-understand book that should be a big help. . . . If you're like me, the cost of the book will easily be worth the hours of frustration saved."

—*Berkshire (MA) Courier*

by Bob Syvanen

Drafting: Tips and Tricks on
Drawing and Designing House Plans

Carpentry and Exterior Finish: Some Tricks of the Trade

Carpentry and Interior Finish: More Tricks of the Trade

Getting a Good House:
Tips and Tricks for Evaluating New Construction

HOME BUILDER'S LIBRARY, VOLUME THREE

Carpentry and Interior Finish:

More Tricks of the Trade from an Old-Style Carpenter

Second Edition

by Bob Syvanen

Old Saybrook, Connecticut

Library of Congress Cataloging-in-Publication Data

Syvanen, Bob.
  Carpentry and interior finish / more tricks of the trade from an
old-style carpenter / by Bob Syvanen. -- 2nd ed.
      p.   cm. -- (Home builder's library ; v. 3)
    Rev. ed. of: Interior finish. 1982.
    ISBN 1-56440-251-7
    1. Finish carpentry--Amateurs' manuals. I. Syvanen, Bob.
Interior finish. II. Title. III. Series.
  TH5640.S98   1993
  694'.6--dc20   93-8771
                                                          CIP

Manufactured in the United States of America
Second Edition/First Printing

Contents

Introduction

This book was done with the same intent as were the carpentry and drafting books: to help and encourage.

Interior finish has as many unforeseen problems as the framing; and unfortunately finish work is very visible. But keep in mind that it is a house you are building and not a piano.

Things are always happening on a job that you hadn't planned on, but the solution is there. Sometimes it's, "Oh yeah, I did something like that back in 1955" and other times it's brand new (to you). Let that inner wisdom find it for you. A little experience can't hurt either, and that's where I hope I can help.

TRANSLATION:
HO BOY, THE TRILOGY IS FINISHED.

The exterior is finished. Now comes the interior.

I do not mention safety practices or devices, assuming that basic procedures would be practiced by the reader. Safety goggles, protective clothing, proper ventilation, and safe ladders are all part of good carpentry. OSHA rules, building codes, manufacturers' instructions, and, above all, good old common sense should be considered in all carpentry jobs.

Of course we timed it so that the bad weather will be spent doing the inside work.

There is a lot of blocking to go in before the finished ceiling and finished walls go on.

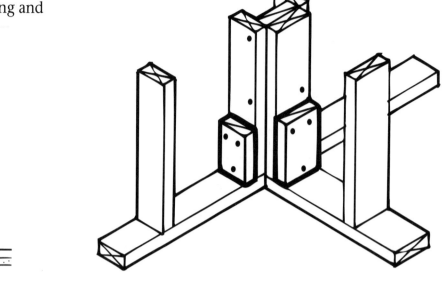

PLAN AT INSIDE CORNER

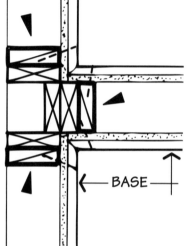

The inside corners need blocking to make nailing the baseboard easier. You won't have to reach into the corner to find nailing.

PLAN AT DOOR

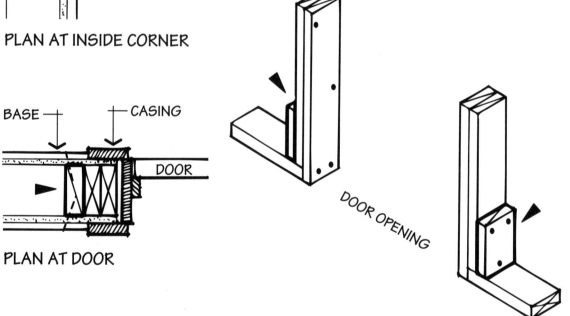

Blocking at door openings is required for the same reason. The casing usually extends past the jamb studs, leaving very little to nail to.

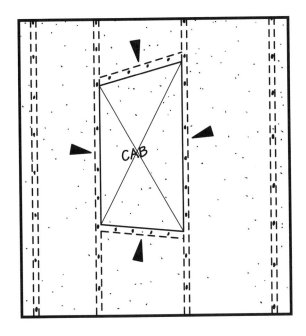

Medicine cabinets are screwed to side blocking, so make sure there is something to screw into. The top and bottom should be blocked, too. It helps to mark the cabinet's location as the Sheetrock goes on; but even if unmarked, it is easy to locate.

1x6 blocking is good enough for towel bars, shower heads, and faucets. It's a good idea to mark these locations on the Sheetrock.

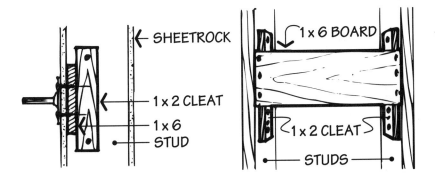

Paneling requires something more substantial.

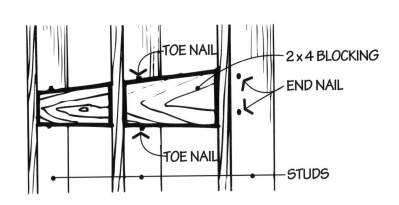

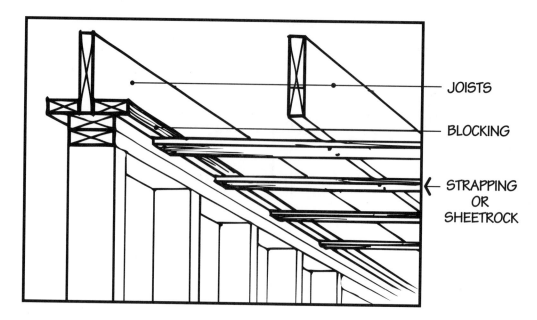

The ceiling should be prepared for either strapping or Sheetrock. Either way, it will need blocking.

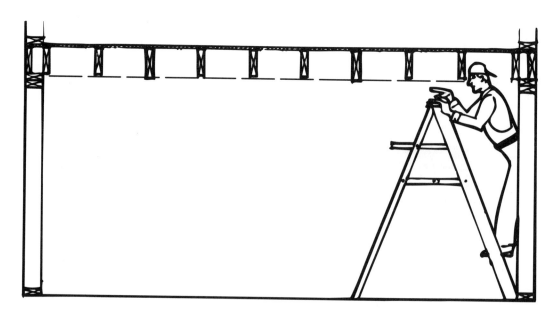

If the Sheetrock is to be installed directly on the joists, eyeball down to see if there are any low-hanging ones. If any need trimming, snap a chalk line and cut with a circular saw or hatchet.

If you can't cut it with a circular saw, a series of cuts across the bottom edge of the joist with a sharp hatchet . . .

followed by strokes parallel to, and at, the chalk line will do a quick and neat job.

A "strongback" might be all that is needed to even up the bottoms, but not this kind of strong back.

A strongback is a 2x6 nailed to a 2x4 and then nailed to the tops of the ceiling joists, pulling any bowed ones into line. A 2x8 can be used for more strength.

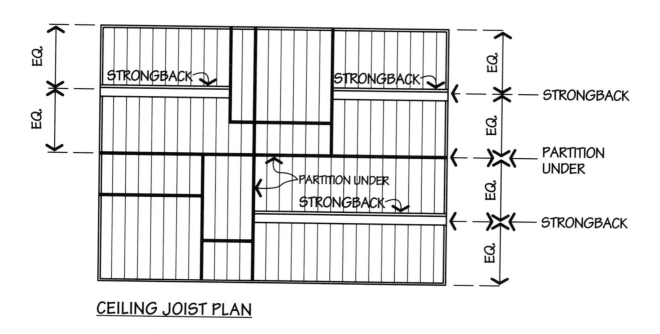

CEILING JOIST PLAN

The strongback is located at midspan and only where the floor space above the joists is not usable.

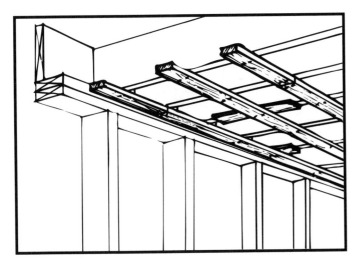

New England is the only place I know of that uses 1x3 strapping as a base for a Sheetrock ceiling. It is a terrific way to get a flat ceiling, but most carpenters just strap the ceiling and then install the Sheetrock without leveling it.

Eyeball for any bad joists and fix before strapping. The easiest way to get the job done is to nail up all the strapping and then eyeball for adjusting. For a super job, work to a stretched string.

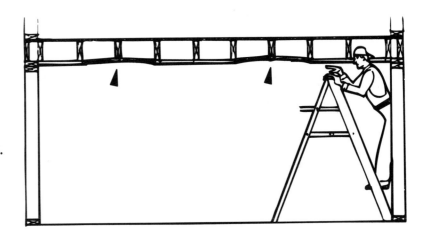

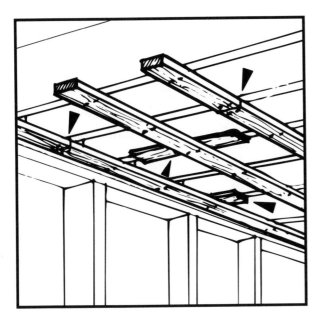

Use shingle tips, between strapping and joists, to adjust. I like to double-nail for a more stable condition, but a single nail will surely hold. When a ceiling needs joints in the strapping, alternate them.

Measure the various size strapping lengths and cut them while the bundle is still tied together.

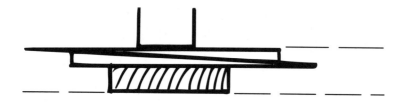

Two shingles used butt to tip makes a better shim job.

One shingle will tip the face. If the face is already tipped, then one shingle can correct it.

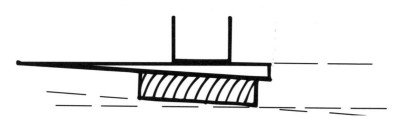

If plaster is to be used, then there is no need to worry about the joist bottoms; the plaster will take care of that. In the old days, the boss would encourage an apprentice to put on a thick coat of plaster by throwing a handful of sand into the skimpy coat already applied.

Check the walls for badly bowed studs by holding a long straight 2x4 against the wall. It will be obvious which ones are bad. A badly bowed stud in a finished wall really shows, so it is wise to replace or straighten it.

To straighten a bowed stud, cut well into it on the side opposite the hump.

The stud can then be pushed to a straight position. Wood-shingle tips driven into the cut will keep the stud straight while cleats are nailed on each side. It might take two such cuts if the bow is bad.

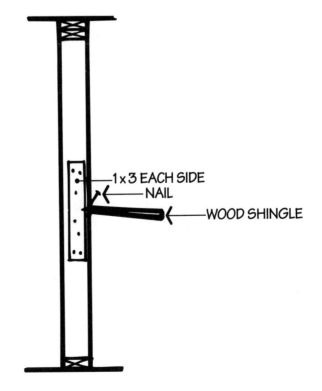

1 x 3 EACH SIDE
NAIL
WOOD SHINGLE

Insulation plays a vital role in finishing a house, particularly in these days of high fuel costs. There are five problem areas that should be done with care: corners, partition intersections, roofs, spaces behind electrical-outlet boxes, and vapor barriers.

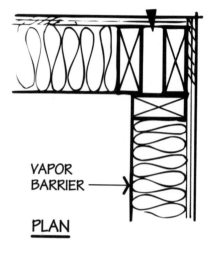

The standard outside corner does not insulate well.

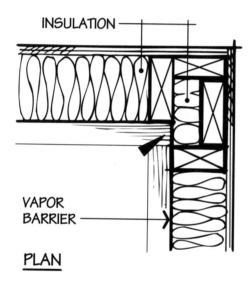

This corner allows for good insulation.

If the "Finnish wall" (Scandinavian) is used and the 2x2s are planted on the face of the studs and parallel, insulate before the 2x2s go on in the corner. If the 2x2s are perpendicular to the studs, there is no problem.

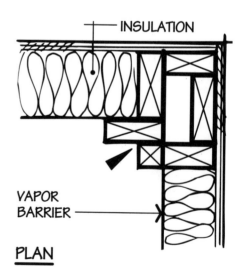

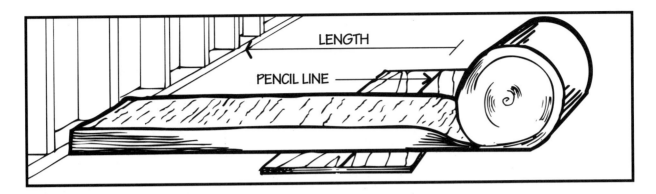

A pencil line on a piece of scrap plywood is a quick, easy guide for duplicate cutting of insulation. Position the plywood so that the pencil line indicates the length each strip of insulation is to be cut.

If there is a paper backing on the insulation, it should be down, with the fluff side up. Compress the insulation with a board that lines up with the pencil line and cut with a sharp utility knife.

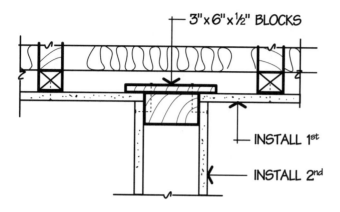

3"x6"x½" BLOCKS

INSTALL 1st

INSTALL 2nd

INSIDE CORNER PLAN

Where a partition butts an exterior wall, I favor Sheetrock clips or 3"x6"x½" plywood blocks at 16 inches on center. This allows for unbroken insulation between studs.

There must be an air space between the top of the insulation and the bottom of the roofing boards to prevent condensation.

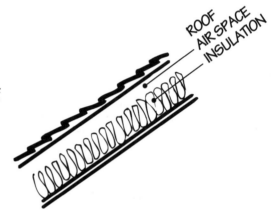

ROOF
AIR SPACE
INSULATION

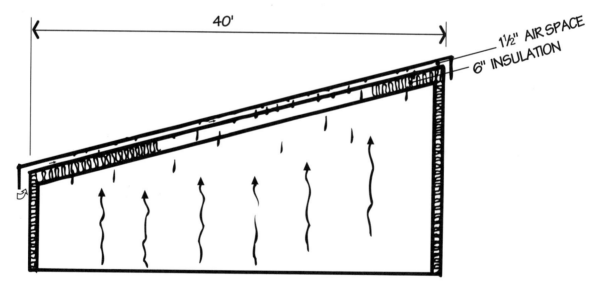

40'

1½" AIR SPACE

6" INSULATION

I have this condition in my house, and it "rains" inside because not enough air moves in the 40-foot roof. The roof is cold; and when the warm air hits it, you wouldn't believe the condensation.

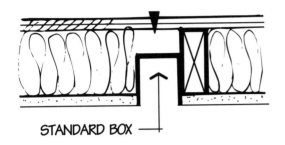

STANDARD BOX

An electrical-outlet box pretty much fills in a 2x4 stud wall. The result is that, directly behind the box, there is no insulation.

The Finnish wall eliminates this problem by keeping the electrical work in the 1½-inch air space. This is not without its problems because of the shallow outlet boxes that must be used. The shallow box gets crowded in a hurry, but junction boxes will help.

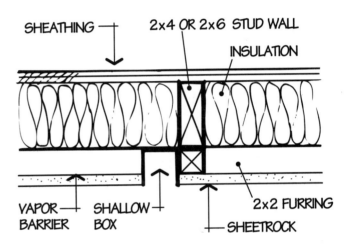

SHEATHING — 2x4 OR 2x6 STUD WALL
INSULATION

VAPOR BARRIER — SHALLOW BOX — 2x2 FURRING — SHEETROCK

THE FINNISH WALL

The Finnish wall also takes care of the vapor-barrier problem. Just 3 percent moisture in insulation reduces its "R" value by 50 percent; so the fewer breaks there are in the vapor barrier, the more efficient the insulation will be.

When sheets of polyethelene are joined, it is best to lock the seam for a good seal.

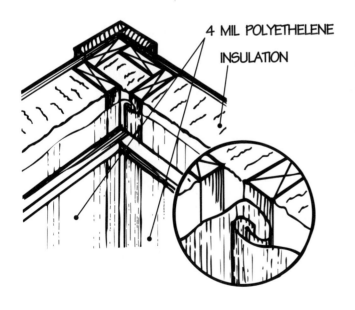

4 MIL POLYETHELENE
INSULATION

A basement wall is best insulated on the outside.

◉ Underlayment

The kitchen and bathroom finished floors are usually vinyl over plywood underlayment. Versa-Board or any composition board is not a good product to use where there is moisture, since it swells when wet. Use plywood, plugged and sanded on one side; it's made for underlayment.

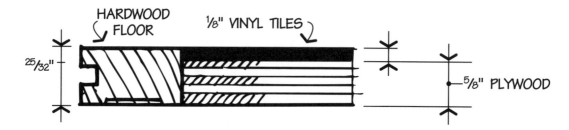

When kitchen or bathroom meets a hardwood floor, ⅝-inch plywood with ⅛-inch tile will make both floors about even.

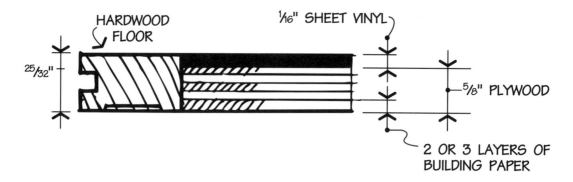

If ¹⁄₁₆-inch sheet of vinyl is used, a few layers of building paper will bring the vinyl surface flush with the hardwood. Try a sample of the plywood, building paper, and vinyl against a piece of flooring. Check the plywood; it's apt to measure anything these days.

With a door closed, the floor of the adjacent room should not be visible.

. . . door swings over vinyl floor

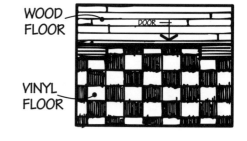

Door swings over wood floor . . .

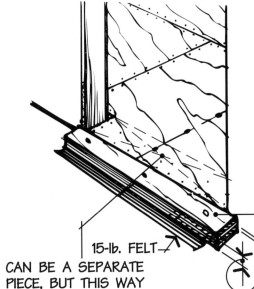

If the vinyl flooring extends around the door jambs, run the underlayment in one piece. There is a lot of traffic in these areas; and the more secure the underlayment is, the less wear there will be on the vinyl. Where the underlayment ends at a door, protect the edge with a piece of plywood nailed against it. It's temporary.

TEMPORARY PROTECTION FOR
EDGE OF UNDERLAYMENT

15-lb. FELT

CAN BE A SEPARATE
PIECE, BUT THIS WAY
IS BETTER.

SAME THICKNESS
AS UNDERLAYMENT

Snap a chalk line on the underlayment over every joist. The underlayment should be nailed through the subfloor into the joists for a secure floor. Use spiral flooring nails at the joists and ring shank nails in between and around the perimeter. If the underlayment has any movement, the nails want to walk out and push through the vinyl, so make sure it is securely nailed. For a really squeak-free floor, use mastic or construction adhesive, spread with a notched trowel, on the underlayment. The 15-lb. felt is not used with this system, but the same nailing is required.

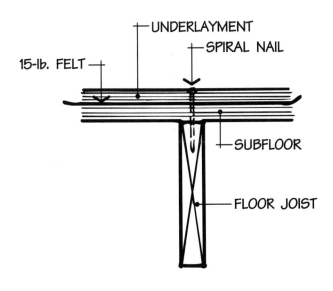

UNDERLAYMENT
SPIRAL NAIL
15-lb. FELT
SUBFLOOR
FLOOR JOIST

RING SHANK NAIL

Both of these nails have good holding power.

SPIRAL FLOORING NAIL

The ceiling is the place to start, and you need two people to do it. I have done the job alone, but I don't recommend it.

This guy is destined for disaster.

A couple of T braces will make the job easier. Be sure you can reach them and still control the sheet overhead. It also helps to stick a few nails in the Sheetrock where the nailing will be. Holding the sheet overhead while fishing for nails can be tough.

The T brace should be a little longer than the floor to ceiling height so that there is a slight wedge fit. If it is too long, the brace won't stay in place; if too short, the whole business comes down.

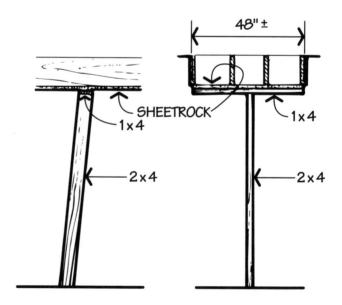

The easiest way to hold a sheet against the ceiling is with your head. The flatter the head, the better.

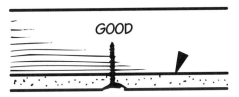

When nailing, make sure the sheet is pushed hard against the joists or strapping before driving the nail home.

If you don't, the nail will pull through the surface of the Sheetrock.

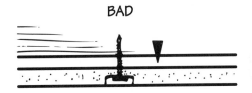

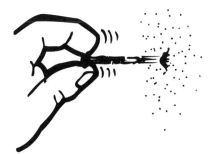

If a nail misses a joist or stud, pull it out.

Hit the hole with a hammer hard enough to depress the surface without breaking the paper.

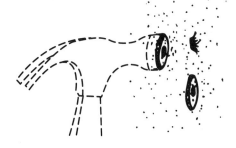

These dents, or dimples, can be filled easily with joint compound.

For a better, faster, and easier drywall hanging system, use drywall (Sheetrock) screws and a drywall screwdriver. The screwdrivers can be rented, cord or cordless, and are well worth the rental fee.

If the ceiling requires a butted joint at the end of a row, it should not land on a joist or strapping. The end is not tapered, and, when taped and spackled, it will show a bad bulge.

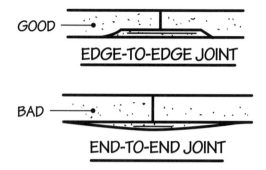

One solution is to nail up blocking at 16 inches on center and then a 2x4 or strapping down the middle, parallel to the joists, so that the Sheetrock will be depressed ⅛ inch. The Sheetrock edges are then nailed or screwed to the 2x4 or strapping.

Another, more common, way is to cut four 12x12-inch squares of Sheetrock.

Butter these pieces with joint compound and slip them in on the back side of the panel already in place.

The next sheet is nailed in place and a piece of strapping is placed along the seam and held in place with cross pieces of strapping. These cross pieces will depress the joint, and the buttered 12x12s will dry holding everything in place. The joint is then taped and spackled like any other.

Working from a ladder or horses is all right, but a simple pair of stilts can be a great help. I've heard that some places have outlawed their use because someone got hurt, so be cautious. I myself wouldn't try hanging sheet using stilts.

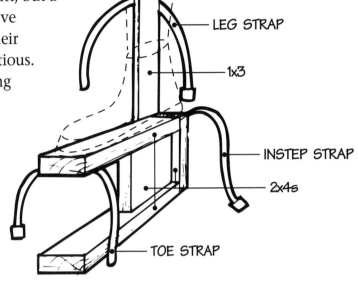

LEG STRAP

1x3

INSTEP STRAP

2x4s

TOE STRAP

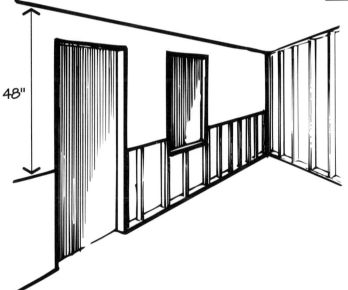

48"

Sheetrock walls are pretty simple. The panel that touches the ceiling should go in first to insure a good joint at the ceiling.

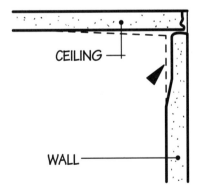

CEILING

WALL

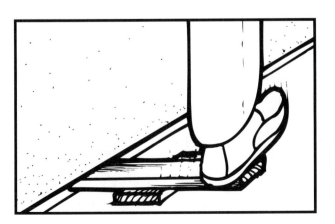

Leave about a ½-inch gap at the floor so that a wedge can be slipped under to push the lower sheet up tight.

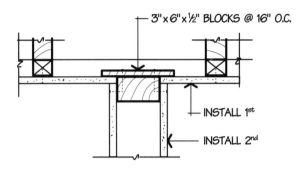

3"x6"x½" BLOCKS @ 16" O.C.

INSTALL 1st

INSTALL 2nd

INSIDE CORNER PLAN

If corner clips or plywood blocks are used at inside corners, install the sheet that runs parallel to the blocks first; no nailing into these blocks or clips is required. The adjacent sheet is nailed to the stud in the corner and holds the first in place. Tape and spackle will keep the corner together.

The only thing to remember about the outside corner is to make sure the Sheetrock extends far enough into the corner so that the corner bead will have backing behind it.

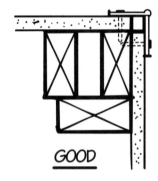

GOOD

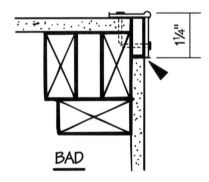

1¼"

BAD

Poor nailing condition here.

When Sheetrocking around doors and windows, run the sheet by in one piece and cut it out for the opening. If pieces are put in over the door or window, it will crack at the seam.

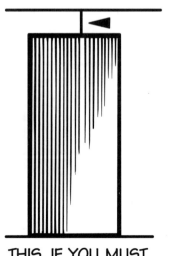

THIS, IF YOU MUST

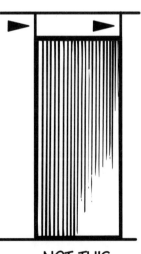

NOT THIS

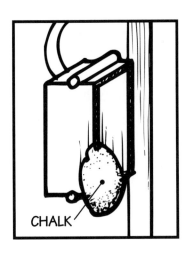

CHALK

Some professional Sheetrockers cover the wall and then cut the outlet and switch holes. A safer way is to rub the outlet box with block chalk, hold the sheet in place, smack it with an open palm, and cut the resulting mark left on the back side of the sheet. Another way is to measure the location and mark it on the sheet—not bad, but be prepared for a few mistakes.

A Stanley Surform is a good tool for shaving a Sheetrock edge. A piece of expanded wire lath wrapped around a block of wood, though, works just as well.

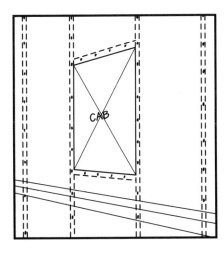

CAB

Don't forget to mark all openings for medicine cabinets, fans, and the like as the sheets go up. They are easily lost.

An aluminum "hawk" can be bought for around $15.00, but a plywood one will work almost as well and is a lot cheaper.

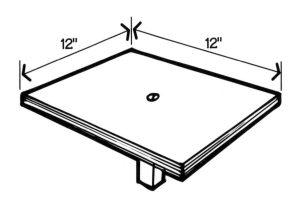

12"   12"

A 60-pound bucket of ready-mix joint compound is very convenient to work with. It's easy to scoop the compound out of.

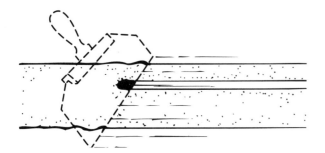

Cleanliness is a must. Any hard lumps or pieces of dirt will mess up a joint, so keep the cover on.

Load up the hawk by scooping compound from the bucket with a wood shingle. Keep the shingle in the bucket and cover to keep moist and clean.

Scrape the trowel clean as you work. If the scrapings are clean and soft, mix it with the stuff on the hawk. Try to keep the compound together so it won't dry out as fast. If there is any problem with it (hard lumps, dirt, etc.), dump it.

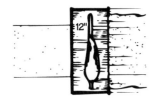 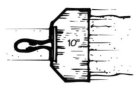 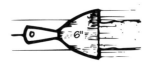 

Four trowels are required to do a good joint job: a 6-inch, 10-inch, and 12-inch, and a corner trowel.

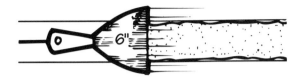

To do a joint, start with a 6-inch trowel and put a layer of compound as wide as the tape the length of the joint.

The trowel held at a flattened angle will leave a nice bed of compound.

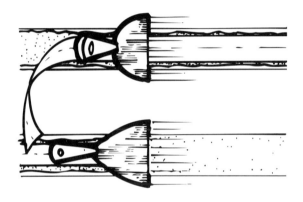

Lay the tape on the compound joint and push it flat with the 6-inch trowel. Get all the bubbles out.

Spread a thin layer of compound over the tape. Keep it smooth; you'll do less sanding that way.

Fiberglass tape with a sticky face eliminates the first step. You just stick it on and then apply a coat of compound. It's a big help when working overhead, but it costs about three times what paper tape does.

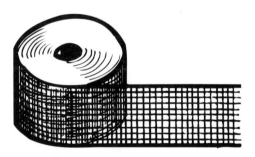

Raise the trowel toward perpendicular for smoothing. Try different angles for the best results.

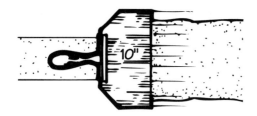

The next coat is done the same way, but with the 10-inch trowel. That is, lay on a coat . . .

. . . wipe the trowel clean . . .

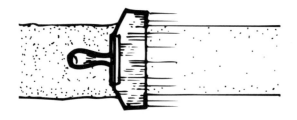

. . . then run the full length of the joint to smooth it out.

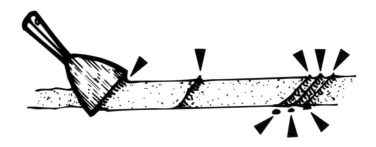

Every time the trowel is picked up from the joint, it pulls some compound with it, leaving a ridge; so try to do the joint in one stroke. Every bump the trowel hits reflects on the surface of the joint. When smoothing out, it may take a few strokes to get the excess off. Make that last stroke a nice one, since it's the base for the next coat.

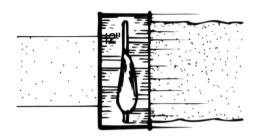

The last coat is done with the 12-inch trowel in the same manner as the others.

Try to make a long, smooth run for this coat.

The 12-inch trowel is much stiffer than the others and has a curved bottom, so it takes a good bit of pressure to smooth and feather out the final coat.

Each coat must be sanded when dry with 80 grit. Sand the last with 120 or finer. The better the joints are feathered, the less sanding will be required. Be sure to wear a good dust-filter mask while sanding.

A good place to use up the semidried compound is in nail holes and dents. Run the trowel at a flattened angle to leave a layer of compound in the dent.

Then hold the trowel almost perpendicular, apply enough pressure to bend its blade, and scrape the surface flat. Go to the next dent, deposit, scrape, next, deposit, and scrape; to the next, deposit, and scrape; and so on.

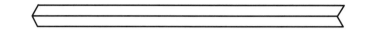

Inside corners are done in a similar fashion, but here the paper tape is prefolded to fit the corner. The tape has a crease down the middle, so folding is easy. There are folding tools available.

The procedure is the same, but use the corner trowel to lay in the first coat of compound . . .

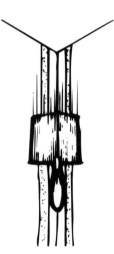

. . . lay in the tape . . .

. . . a coat of compound, and sand. Then smooth on a finish coat of compound.

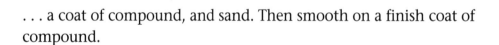

Exterior corners are the easiest of all. Nail on the metal corner bead and compound the joints with the 6-inch trowel.

There will be excess compound running around the corner as you trowel, but not to worry. It's easy to scrape and sand the metal corner.

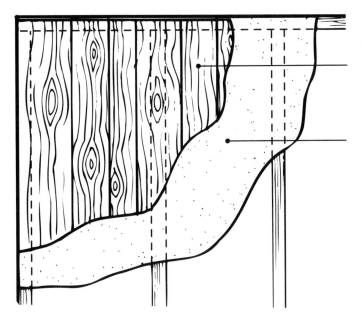

If a wall is to be covered with plywood panel sheets, the best installation is over ⅜-inch Sheetrock. It's solid and makes for better sound proofing.

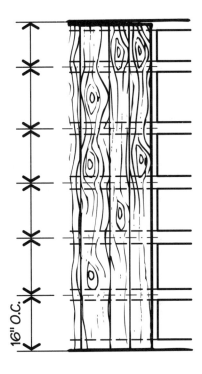

The next best way is on horizontal strapping (16 inches on center).

30" TO 40"

30" TO 40"

If applied directly to studs, block the studs at 30 to 40 inches from top and bottom.

YAK YAK YAK...

This will protect the areas where bumping occurs.

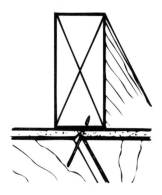

When nailing in the V groove, nail through the side of the V at a slight angle; it holds better.

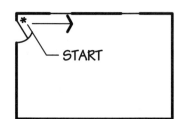

With any trim, look for ways to hide joints. With paneling, the last piece is the toughest to fit, so look for a good place to hide it. A door or window near a corner is a good place to make that last joint.

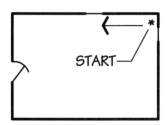

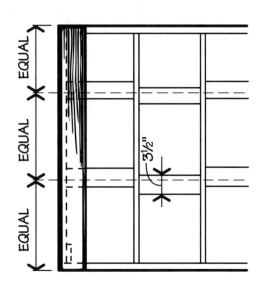

With solid ¾-inch paneling laid up vertically, 2x4 horizontal blocking is needed. If the blocks are put in flat and staggered, they are easier to nail, and it leaves a straight line of wood to nail into. You don't have to guess where the nailing is.

Before any paneling is nailed up, it is a good idea to spread it around the room so it can be looked over. Match the paneling, look for very dark or light; pick out odd-looking ones. Cut up those that don't blend in and use them for trim.

Back prime if there is a moisture problem.

If the panels are to be painted or stained dark, it is a good idea to paint the tongues so they won't show when the boards shrink.

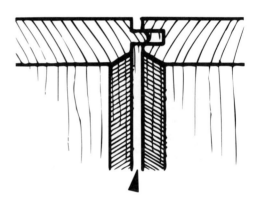

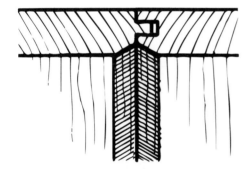

The joints don't always stay like this.

Use a scrap piece of paneling (the groove edge) as a block to hammer against and drive each panel up tight.

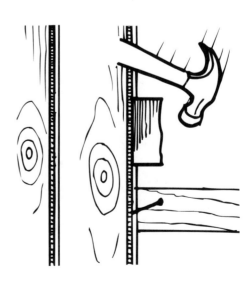

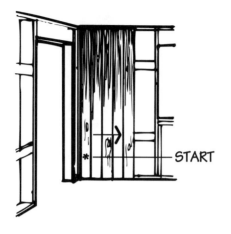

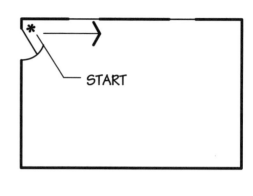

Start in a corner that will make the last piece easy to install.

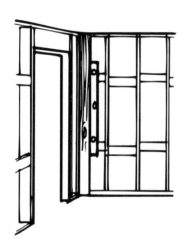

Plumb and, if necessary, scribe the first board to fit the corner. Toenail just above the tongue at the blocking and set these nails. Face nail at the top and bottom where the base and molding will cover nails.

There is no great mystery to nailing each panel, but do check the plumb once in a while and adjust.

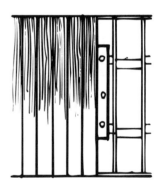

To aid in driving a stubborn board over, start a nail with the tongue edge of a panel raised slightly.

PLUMB

PLUMB

Inside corners will have to be scribed with the board held in the plumb position.

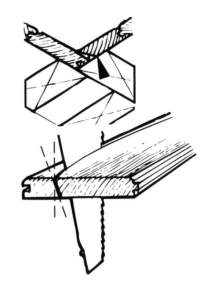

Rip with a handsaw and back-cutting for a tight fit in front.

The outside corner is mitered and relieved at the back of the miter so that the front of the miter will be tight.

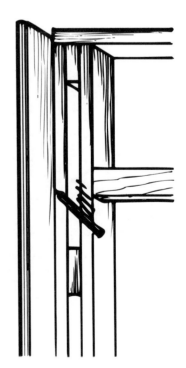

If the next to the last piece of panel at an outside corner is plumb (and it should be), take the longest measurement to the corner and use it for a parallel 45-degree-plus cut on the table saw. If the corner is badly out of plumb, it will have to be measured top and bottom for this cut.

Transfer the marks on the back to the front with a 45-degree combination square and rip with a handsaw.

A sharp ripsaw does this job nicely.

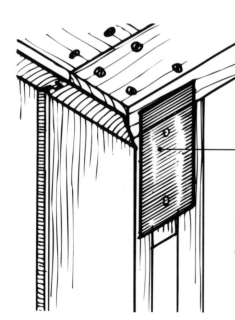

BUILDING PAPER FOR SHIMMING

If an outside corner isn't perfect, a little fudging can be done with building-paper shims.

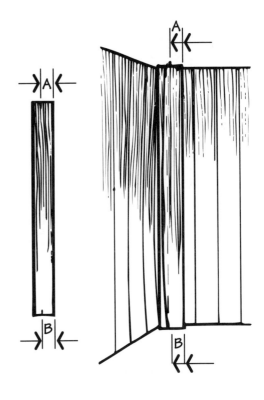

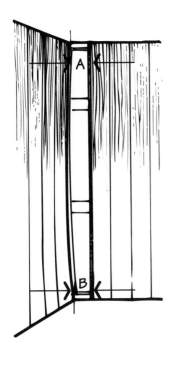

For an inside corner, the last space is measured top and bottom.

Mark the panel, tack in place parallel to the next-to-last board, and scribe.

This scribed line is ripped with a sharp ripsaw. Be sure to back-cut it.

When working with paneling, be extra careful about keeping hands clean. It's easier than cleaning the paneling.

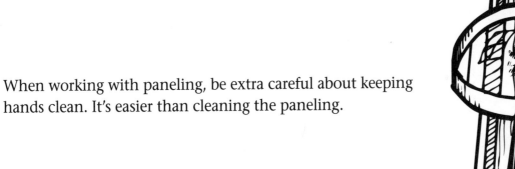

More real finish work: door frames. There are two things to consider here: style and width.

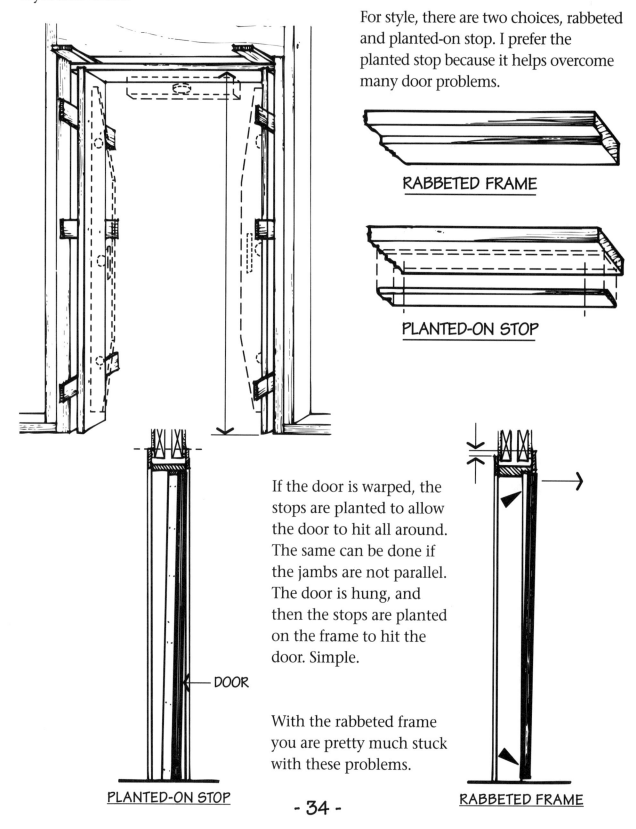

For style, there are two choices, rabbeted and planted-on stop. I prefer the planted stop because it helps overcome many door problems.

RABBETED FRAME

PLANTED-ON STOP

If the door is warped, the stops are planted to allow the door to hit all around. The same can be done if the jambs are not parallel. The door is hung, and then the stops are planted on the frame to hit the door. Simple.

With the rabbeted frame you are pretty much stuck with these problems.

DOOR

PLANTED-ON STOP

RABBETED FRAME

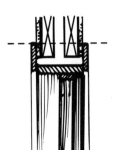

Another good reason for the planted-on stop is that, on both sides of the door, the head casings will always be at the same level.

Not so with the rabbeted frame:

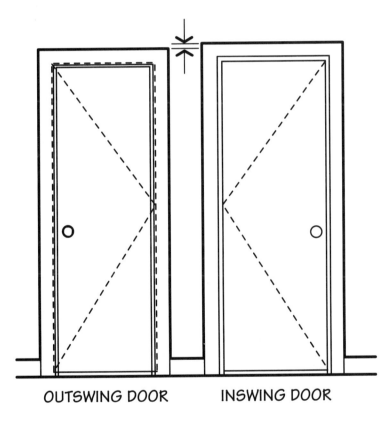

OUTSWING DOOR   INSWING DOOR

The inside is higher than the outside with the rabbeted frame.

The width is decided by measuring from face of Sheetrock to face of Sheetrock at the door openings. You will be surprised at the variations, not only from door to door, but also top to bottom and side to side. Of course, the more carefully the framing was done, the fewer the problems like this that will occur. A good framer is worth two finish men.

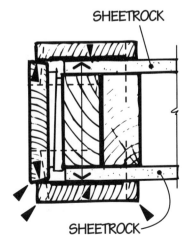

SHEETROCK

SHEETROCK

The frames should be a tad wider than the measurement decided on and beveled back on both edges.

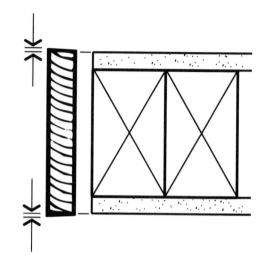

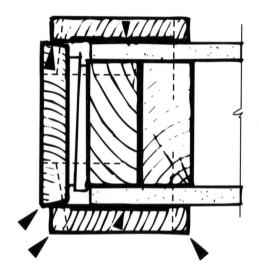

This will allow for a good joint between the casing and the frame. A sharp planer blade on a table saw does a good job. As the pieces are beveled, mark the inside face so that the right face will be grooved for the head frame and the frame will be assembled properly.

There is also a choice when putting frames together. Either groove out the jambs to receive the header . . .

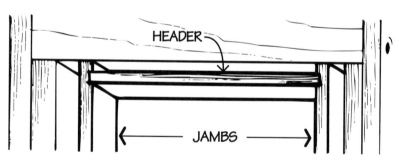

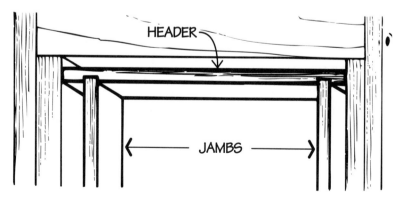

. . . or groove out the header to receive the jambs. I prefer to groove the header; it's more stable in the rough opening.

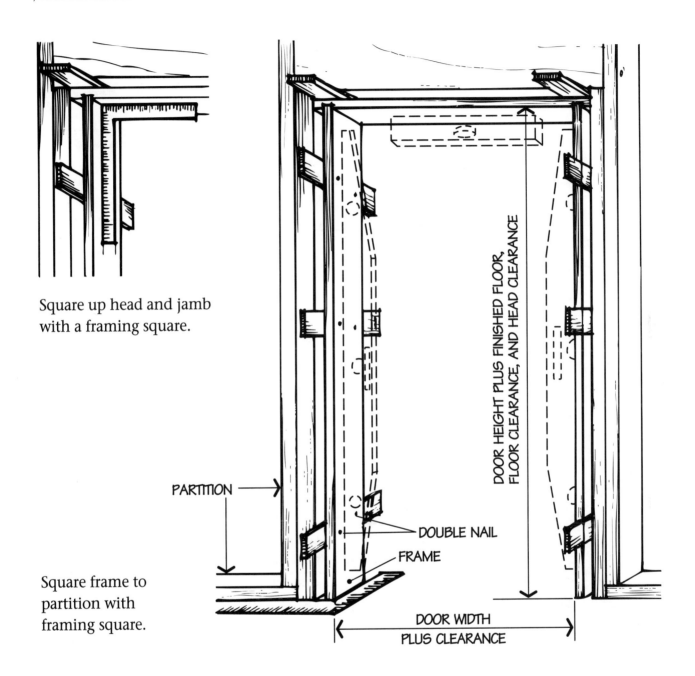

Square up head and jamb with a framing square.

Square frame to partition with framing square.

PARTITION

DOUBLE NAIL

FRAME

DOOR HEIGHT PLUS FINISHED FLOOR, FLOOR CLEARANCE, AND HEAD CLEARANCE

DOOR WIDTH PLUS CLEARANCE

It's a good idea to cut all the headers and jambs for the frames at the same time. Cut them a little longer than required and trim to fit later. The jambs will all be the same length: the door height plus the depth of the groove in the header, header clearance, threshold clearance, and finished-floor thickness. The headers should be at least 1 inch longer than the rough-opening width and cut to fit after assembly.

The grooves in the header are best cut with a dado blade on the table saw, but a knife, handsaw, and chisel will do a fine job.

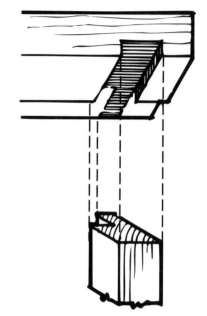

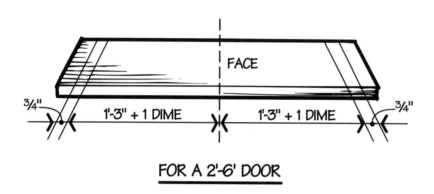

3/4"   1'-3" + 1 DIME   1'-3" + 1 DIME   3/4"

FACE

FOR A 2'-6' DOOR

Start from the center of the header and mark right and left one-half the door width plus the clearance required.

If it is a handsaw-and-chisel job, start by scoring with a sharp knife along a combination square before cutting with a sharp finish saw. This will give a nice, clean, positive line. Cut both sides of the groove only as deep as required (about ¼ inch) before chiseling.

Use the finished header as a pattern for making duplicate headers. There's less chance for error that way.

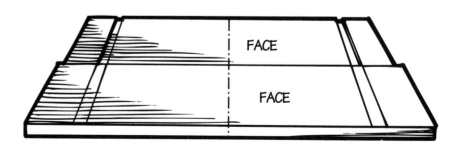

FACE

FACE

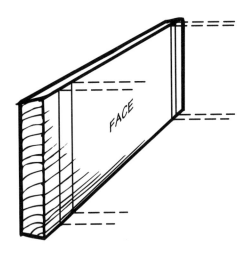

Before grooving and assembling, check for what face goes where; it's easy to mess up here.

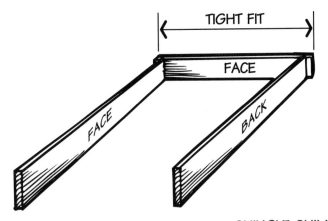

With the frame assembled, cut the header for a tight fit in the rough opening.

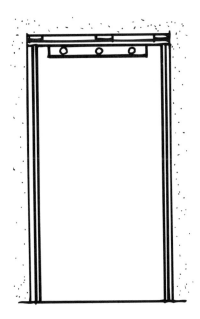

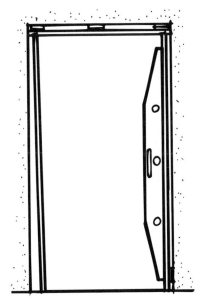

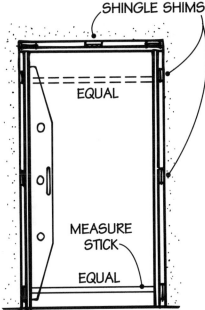

Slip the whole business into the opening and level the header by shimming the bottoms of the jambs. Once it is leveled, snug it down by wedging shingle tips directly over the jambs.

Shim the bottom side of one jamb until plumb using a jamb level (a great tool for door work). A regular six-foot level will work. Then shim the middle to a straight line.

The opposite jamb can then be shimmed over parallel by using a cut-to-size measuring stick.

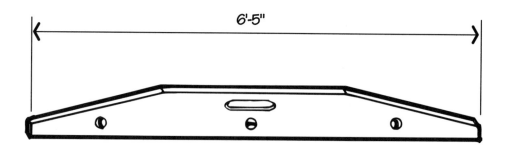

6'-5"

This door-jamb level is also a straightedge.

When shimming with shingles, use two opposing each other except when the framing behind is twisted. In such cases you might need two in the same direction to make the trim piece come square with the work.

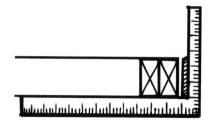

Use a framing square at the base of the opening to square the jamb frame with the wall.

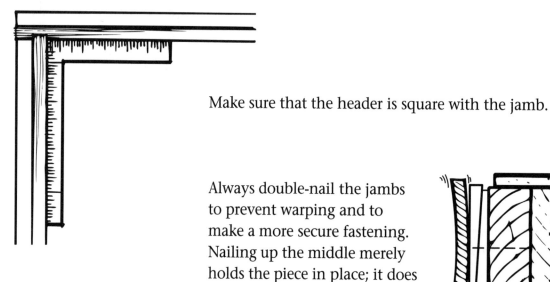

Make sure that the header is square with the jamb.

Always double-nail the jambs to prevent warping and to make a more secure fastening. Nailing up the middle merely holds the piece in place; it does not securely fasten it.

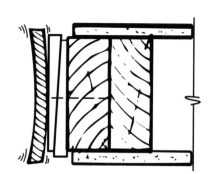

If the doors haven't been prehung, now is the time to hang them. There should be good clearance on each side, top, and bottom:

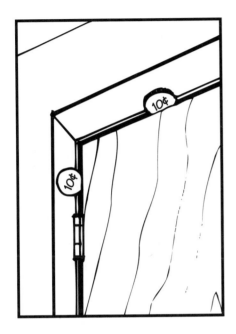

about one dime's thickness at the top and sides if the door is to be stained,

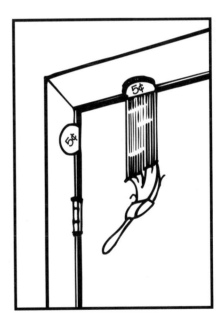

about one nickel's thickness at the top and sides if the door is to be painted,

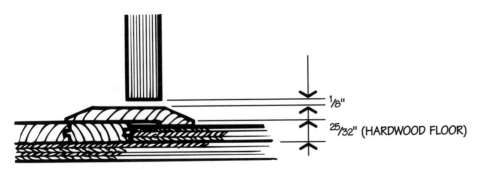

one-eighth inch plus the finished floor and threshold if one is to be used.

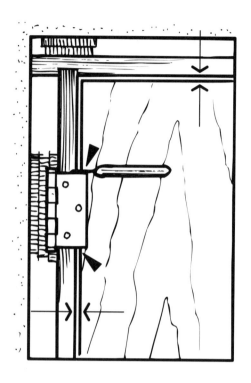

If all is square and plumb, the door should fit with no trouble. Some temporary stop pieces will hold the door in place while marking the butt locations. Shim the door to the proper height and mark the jamb and door with a sharp knife.

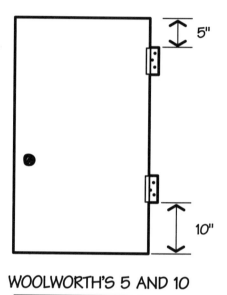

WOOLWORTH'S 5 AND 10

The door butts (hinges) are usually set at 5 inches and 10 inches. I always think of Woolworth's 5 & 10 Store as a reminder.

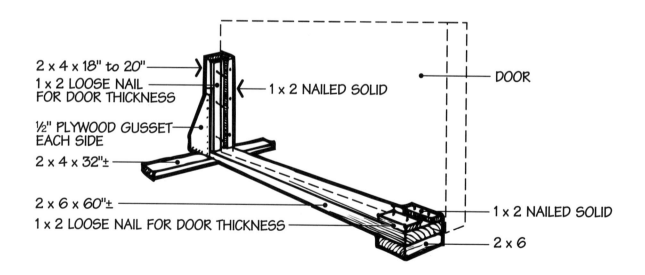

2 x 4 x 18" to 20"
1 x 2 LOOSE NAIL FOR DOOR THICKNESS
1 x 2 NAILED SOLID
DOOR
½" PLYWOOD GUSSET EACH SIDE
2 x 4 x 32"±
2 x 6 x 60"±
1 x 2 LOOSE NAIL FOR DOOR THICKNESS
1 x 2 NAILED SOLID
2 x 6

A door jack is a great help when working on doors. Some carpenters use two 2x4x32 feet, but I find the second one a foot tripper. The jack simply supports the door in a solid vertical position.

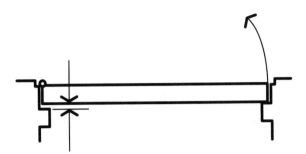

Hinge binding, a big problem with doors, can easily be avoided if enough clearance is left between the doorstop and the door.

If the door is hinge-bound, the hinge must be moved away from the stop or the stop moved away from the door.

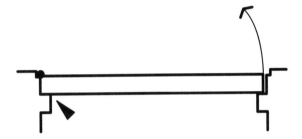

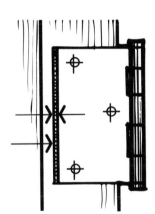

If the hinge is moved back, a wood shim should be laid in to fill the gap and to keep the hinge in place.

OPEN SESAME

LATCH EDGE

If a door is not plumb, it will either want to open by itself or stay closed.

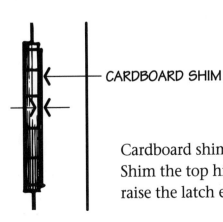

CARDBOARD SHIM

Cardboard shims behind the hinge will change the hang of the door. Shim the top hinge to lower the latch edge, shim the bottom hinge to raise the latch edge.

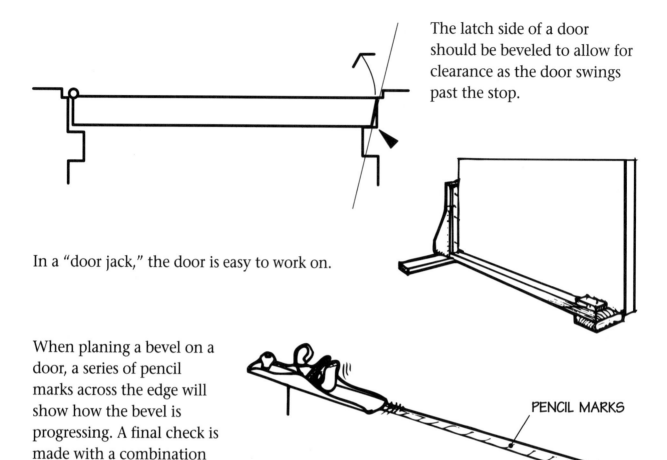

The latch side of a door should be beveled to allow for clearance as the door swings past the stop.

In a "door jack," the door is easy to work on.

When planing a bevel on a door, a series of pencil marks across the edge will show how the bevel is progressing. A final check is made with a combination square.

PENCIL MARKS

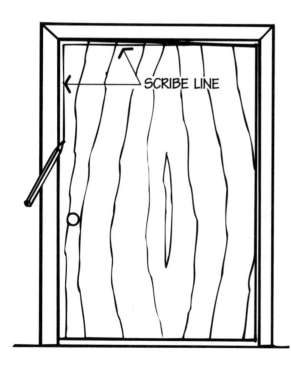

SCRIBE LINE

If the door has proper clearance on the hinge side and hits the header or the opposite jamb, the door must be planed to fit. Close the door as far as it will go and scribe with a pencil, allowing for clearance. Pull the hinge pins, put the door in the door jack, and plane it down.

For setting locks, borrow or rent a lock-boring kit that is made for the lockset being installed. Lumber yards have these. Otherwise, it's measure and drill with a brace and bit.

I have put a lot of hinges on with a combination square, a sharp knife, and a sharp chisel.

The outline is cut to the depth of the hinge.

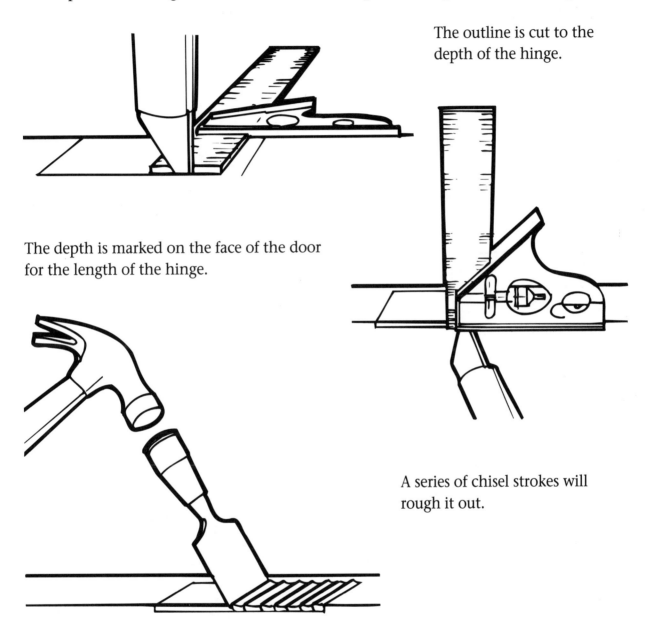

The depth is marked on the face of the door for the length of the hinge.

A series of chisel strokes will rough it out.

With the chisel held flat, the job is finished off. When I work a chisel with my hands, I work with restraint. One hand guides while the other pushes. A sharp tool can be controlled easier than a dull one.

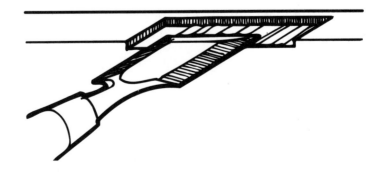

Stanley makes a butt-marking tool that combines all three steps in one tool. One arm sets for the width, the other for the depth. This scribing tool has sharp edges for cutting the outline, like the knife and square setup. The chisel work is still required.

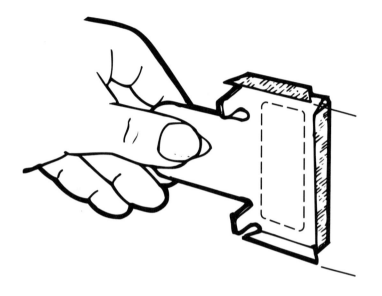

Stanley also makes a butt marker that is put in place and hit with a hammer. The sharp edges leave the outline ready for chiseling. It comes in many sizes.

All these tools are good, but the very best system for doing many doors is the router and butt template guide. Once set up, jambs and doors are routed quickly and accurately. The guide is expensive and cannot be rented.

Butts are set with the edge about ¼ inch from the face of the door, and the screws are offset in the holes to force the butt against this edge.

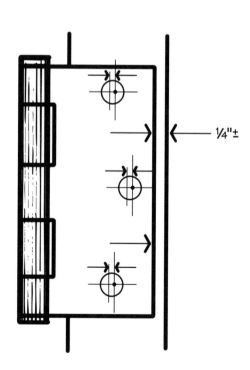

¼"±

Now for some exciting finish work: casings. Mark the reveal on the edge of the frames with a combination square as a guide. Better still, make up a marking gauge from a piece of ¾-inch pine. The combination square is apt to slip, making some funny-looking reveals.

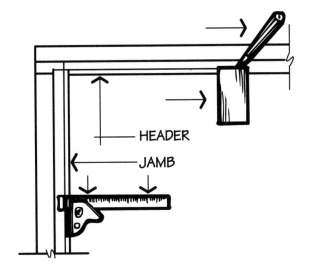

WINDOW OR DOOR FRAME

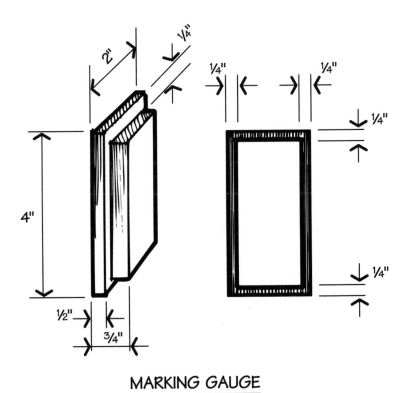

MARKING GAUGE

The wood gauge is always the same, and it frees the combination square for other jobs. The usual reveal is about ¼ inch, but suit yourself.

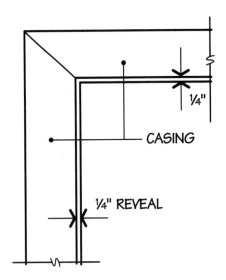

CASING

¼" REVEAL

The two basic choices with casings are mitered and square corners, and they are more easily fitted if the backs are relieved.

This is particularly helpful on bad walls. If square corner casings are used, they cannot be relieved to the ends because they show (unless the corners are mitered).

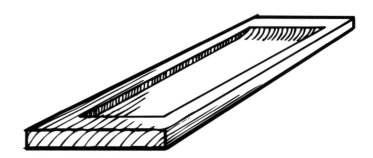

The easiest way to relieve the casings is with a dado blade on a table saw. The mitered casings are run right through, but the square ones are started short and ended short.

The best tool for trim work is an electric miter box. You can't beat it for speed and accuracy. If a thin shaving is required, there is no better way than with this tool.

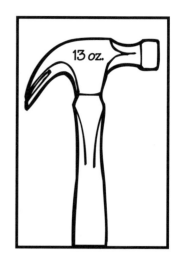

Most carpenters carry one 16-ounce hammer, and it will do for any and all jobs, even fine finish work. Still, I prefer a 13-ounce for finish work; the control is so much better. These hammers are not so easy to find these days, but the best supply houses will carry them.

If the casings go on before the floor, slip a loose piece of flooring under the casing before any measurements are taken. Square the bottom of the side casings by holding them against the reveal line and scribing to the floor.

Start on one side casing and mark the height with a sharp knife at the reveal line on the head frame.

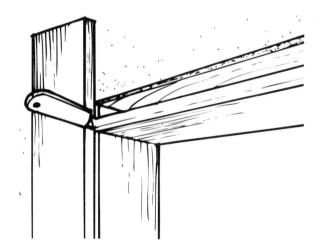

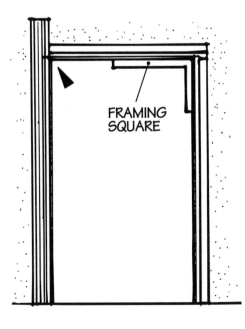

FRAMING SQUARE

If the head and jamb are square then, for a square casing (non-mitered), a square cut at the top of the side casing will work. If they are not square, then a trial cut, a little longer than the reveal mark, is made, and a trial fit with the head casing follows. When the trial fit is right, repeat it at the proper length on the side casing. Tack it in place.

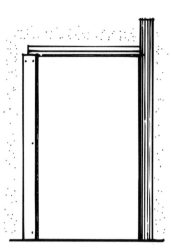

Repeat for the other side casing.

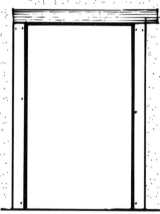

Square-cut one end of the head casing, hold in place, and mark with a sharp knife. Cut and hold in place to check the fit.

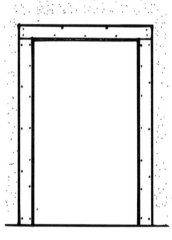

The finished product

Before nailing in place, I like to run a bead of glue on the back of the casing where it touches the frame and where the header sits on the side casings. Be careful if the wood is to be stained, because stain will not take on a glued surface.

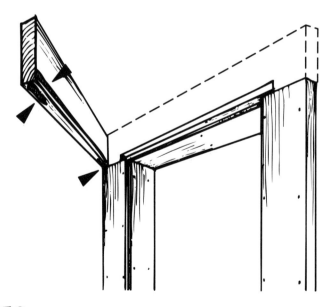

You can, of course, cut all the pieces to the right lengths, nail, sand, and fill the gaps, and it might look all right. But if the trim is to be stained, it never will look good unless you custom-fit each casing.

If there is bad framing at the opening, it can be overcome by shimming or shaving the back of the casing. Here is where the relieving on the backside of the casings helps.

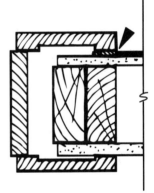

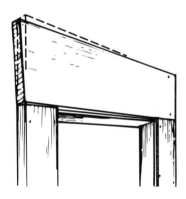

If the head casing tips back . . .

. . . a wedge-shaped shim will make it right. It is always best when the face of the casings are on the same plane.

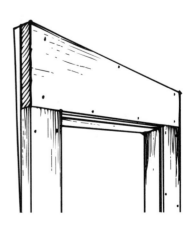

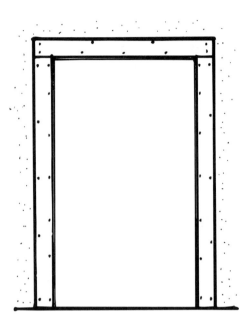

Use 8d finish or casing nails at the outer edge and 4d or 6d at the inner edge. Use as many nails as are required to fasten the trim securely in place.

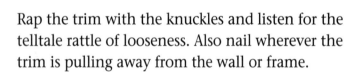

Rap the trim with the knuckles and listen for the telltale rattle of looseness. Also nail wherever the trim is pulling away from the wall or frame.

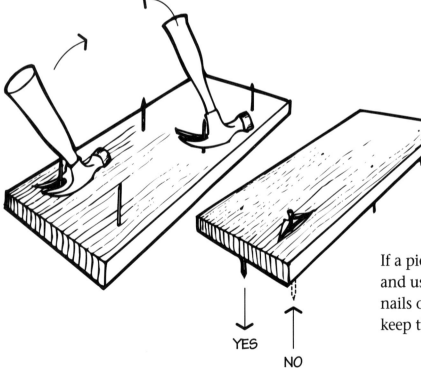

YES

NO

If a piece of trim must be pulled and used again, don't drive the nails out. Pull them through to keep the face clean.

The mitered casing is started the same way as the square casing: by marking the reveal line on the frame.

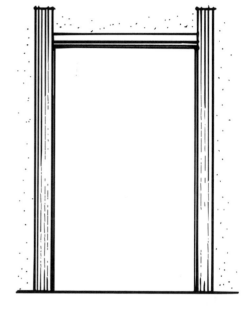

The side casing sits on the finished floor, or blocks simulating the finished floor, and is scribed to fit.

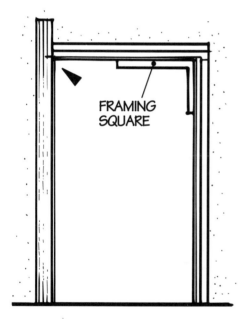

FRAMING SQUARE

Make sure the header is square with the jamb, and mark the header reveal line on one side casing.

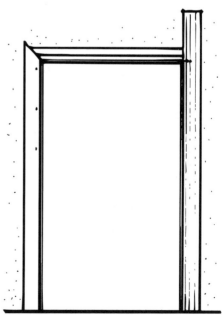

If all is square, then a 45-degree cut is made and the casing is tacked in place.

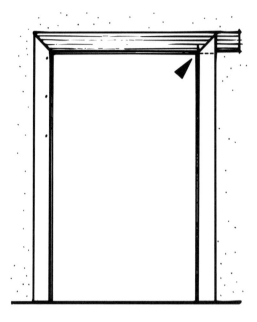

Cut a 45-degree angle on a piece of header stock. Hold in place and, if it needs correcting, shave it with the miter box or a sharp block plane. Hold the trim piece securely while planing; you make cleaner cuts that way. When the fit is good, mark for length at the side-frame reveal line.

Put wedges of whatever thickness at the right or left end of the piece of trim in the miter box to get the desired angle.

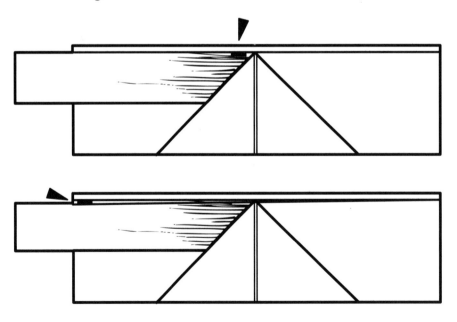

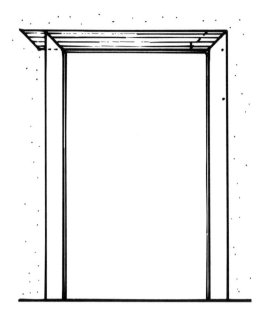

Make a trial cut past the mark and see how it fits. When the fit is good, duplicate the cut at the correct length

A mitered joint must be made up of pieces cut on equal angles or you get an odd corner. You can fudge a little, though, especially if the trim is to be painted.

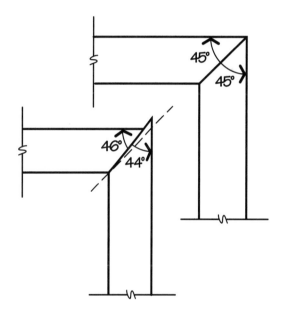

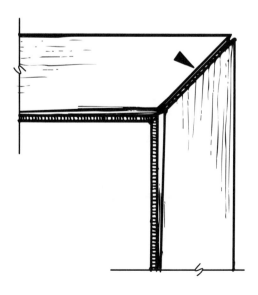

If the header is tipped back, the miter will be open at the face.

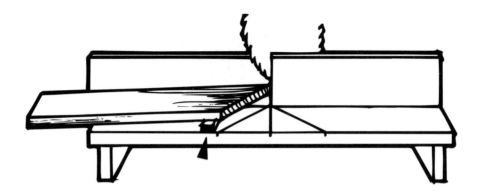

If it is not too bad, it can be corrected by raising (shimming) the piece in the miter box at the saw-blade end. This will relieve the back edge of the miter. Glue it the same as the square casing, including the miter.

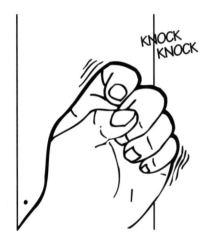

Nail the trim securely and test by knocking.

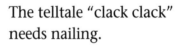

The telltale "clack clack" needs nailing.

If the trim is to be painted, sand the joints with a piece of sandpaper wrapped around a block of wood while the glue is still wet. A better tool is a small random orbital sander. The dust will fill in nicely, making an invisible joint. Stained work must fit without sanding because every scratch will show after staining.

Window casing is basically similar to door casing. The window frame has to be packed out or planed back to the interior-wall face.

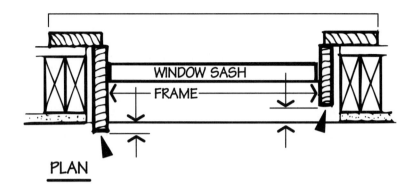

PLAN

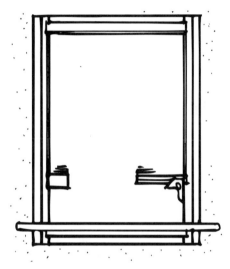

Then, if there is a reveal, it is marked on the frame.

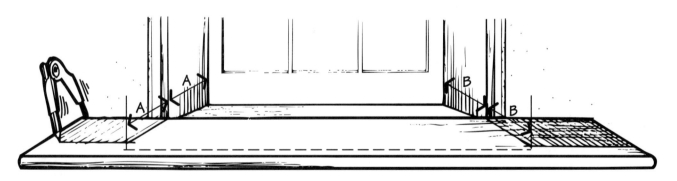

The stool is then scribed to fit against the wall and window, with a little bit of gap at the window to allow for paint and window clearance (1/32-inch minimum).

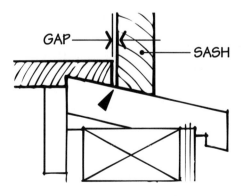

The stool length will be about ¾-inch past the side casings, so keep the rough piece plenty long. The stool piece might have to be ripped to extend no more than ¾-inch past the face of the casing and apron.

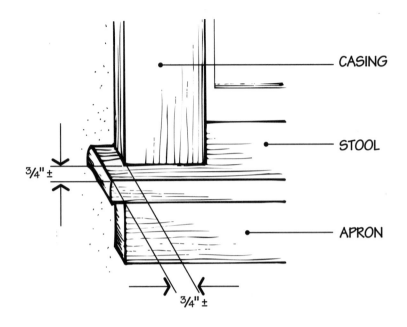

CASING

STOOL

APRON

¾" ±

¾" ±

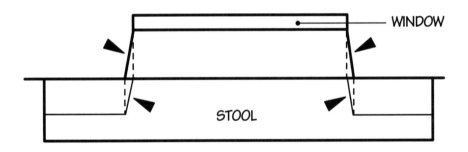

WINDOW

STOOL

The cut parallel to the jamb is marked.

Cut the two notches and tack the stool in place.

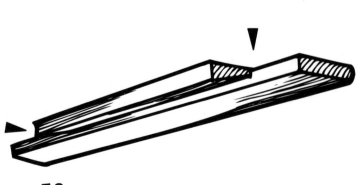

Now the side casings are cut on the bottoms to fit the stool. They should be square cuts. The top cuts are marked . . .

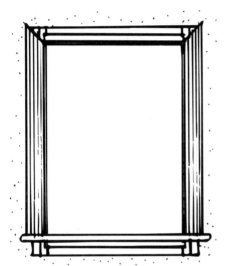

. . . and cut.

One side casing is tacked in place, and a trial header end is cut and fitted. The opposite end is marked for length.

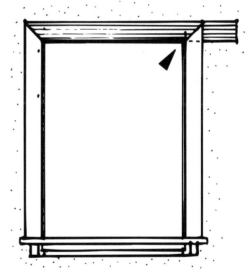

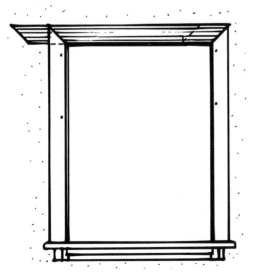

The other end is trial cut and fitted.

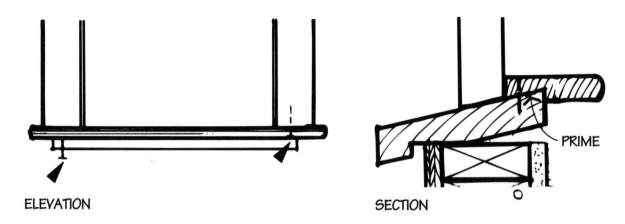

ELEVATION   SECTION   PRIME

The stool is nailed in place first, then the casings. It's a good idea to prime the underside of the stool, which sits on the windowsill. Drive a nail from the bottom of the stool up into each of the side casings.

The apron reaches from outside of casing to outside of casing.

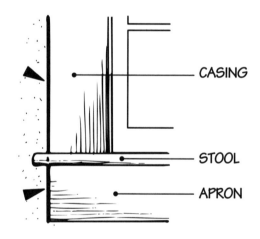

CASING

STOOL

APRON

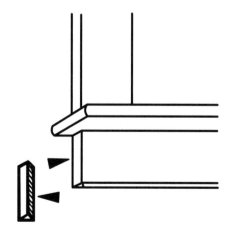

If trim is stained, cut a 45-degree return at each end of the apron. End grain stains darker than face grain.

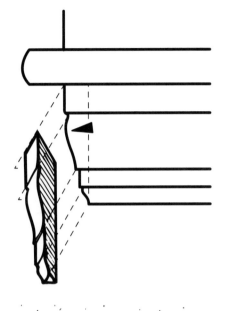

If the trim is molded, shape the return with a coping saw when trim is to be painted. Otherwise, a 45-degree return piece should be fitted.

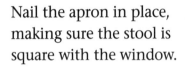

Nail the apron in place, making sure the stool is square with the window.

The finished product

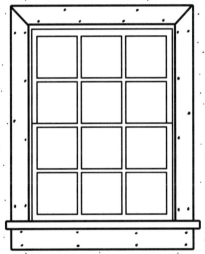

A neat piece of equipment to use for casing work is the "cricket." It's light, the right height, and stable; and it has a shelf for carrying tools and things around on. More on this tidbit later.

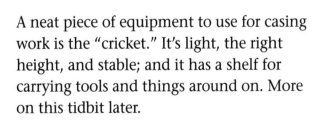

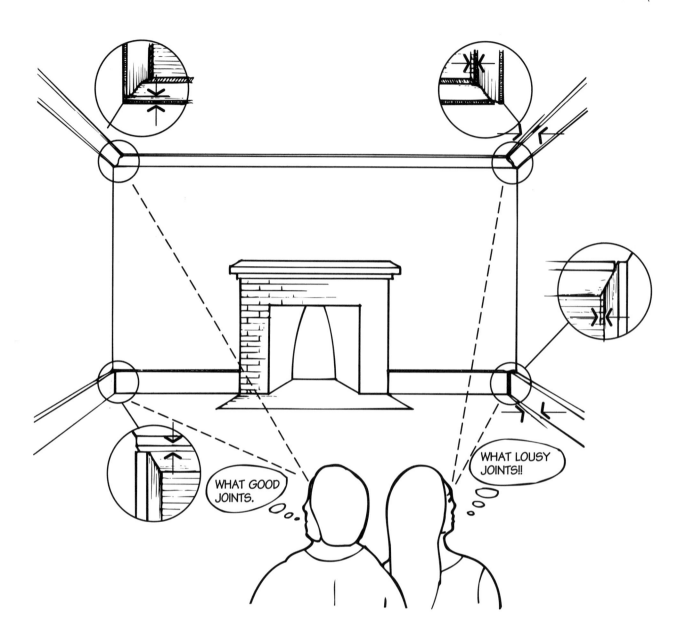

When putting in baseboard or ceiling trim, keep in mind what you see when entering a room and make the joints in such a way that they look good no matter how bad they might be. In this case the joints on both sides of the room are bad, but the joints on the right are obvious and the ones on the left are not.

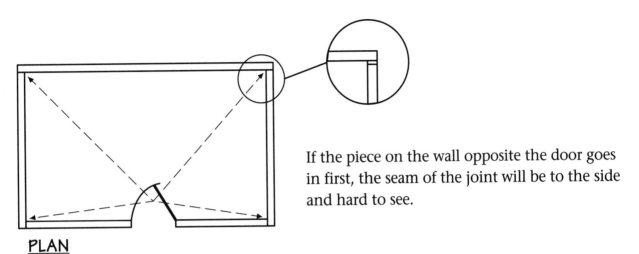

PLAN

If the piece on the wall opposite the door goes in first, the seam of the joint will be to the side and hard to see.

The best joint is a coped joint. There is a buildup of joint compound in the corners, so they are rarely square. The coped corner, when snapped in place, is a very tight fit.

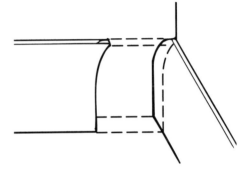

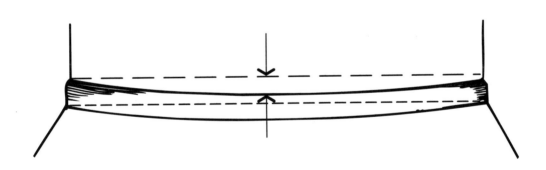

Oops, a little snug.

With the coped corner, the first piece in is cut square on each end and a tad long. The piece is bowed away from the wall at the center and pushed into place at the ends. If the piece is the right length, it will gently snap from your hand when the center is moved closer to the wall. If it is too long, it just won't go at all; if it is a little (as opposed to a tad) too long, the Sheetrock corner will crack.

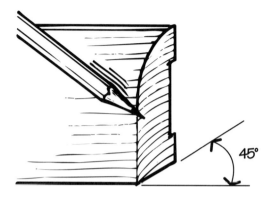

The next piece is cut at a 45-degree angle as if it were a mitered corner. Rub a pencil on the front corner of this miter so that it will be easier to follow with the coping saw (hence the "coped corner").

Start the coping saw on the top, at 90 degrees or perpendicular to the back and, as you follow the penciled corner, ease the saw back from perpendicular to about 87 degrees. Or start on the bottom at 87 degrees and work toward the top, easing over to 90 degrees.

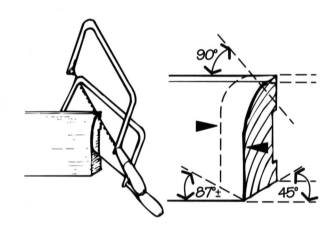

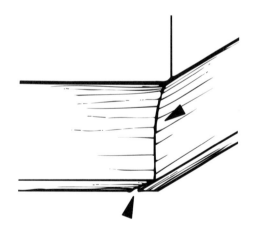

This will ensure that the front edge will hit hard against the adjacent piece of baseboard. Measure from the face of the baseboard already in place to the opposite wall and mark this on the coped piece. Add a little to make a snap fit. It's really simple, but it might take a few practice cuts to get the hang of it.

Even intricate molding shapes can be cut this way. Ceiling molding is done the same way.

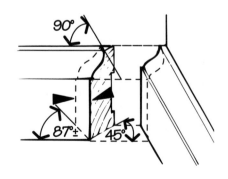

The best-looking corner for square base is the combination mitered-and-coped joint. This square base usually has a rounded upper corner.

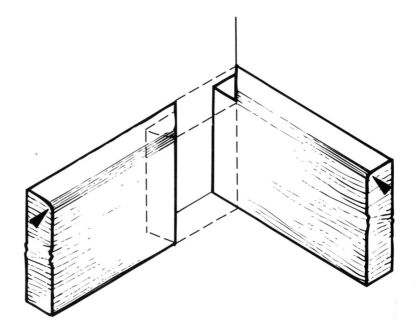

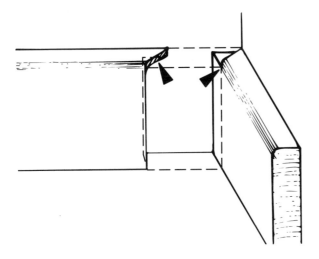

The first piece is square cut and then mitered for about ⅛ inch at the top (to the bottom of the round corner). The adjacent piece is mitered and then cut, from the bottom, up to the bottom of the round corner. Back-cut for a tight fit in front. Cut across with a knife, and there remains about a ⅛-inch miter lip.

Baseboard is nailed at the studs, top and bottom. Sometimes the base is not tight against the wall between studs, but we shall overcome. Use 16d finish nails high on the base and angle down to reach the 2x4 plate. When the nail is set, it should pull the base in.

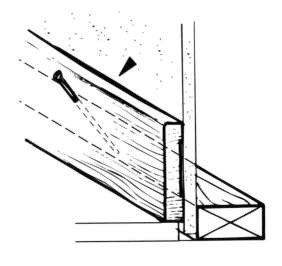

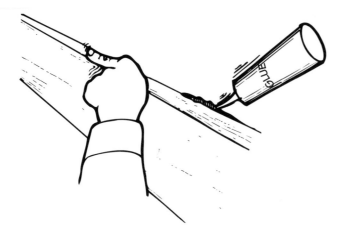

If there is still a space between base and wall, squeeze some glue in and smooth with a finger. It might take a few coats. Don't use this method if the trim is to be stained.

When a "duck puddle" is created with a poorly aimed hammer, just put a dab of saliva in the dent, a double dab if the dent is deep. (If you are chewing tobacco, use a friend.)

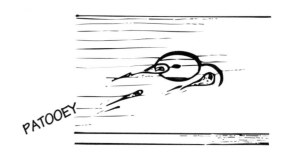

PATOOEY

Drill . . . nail . . . set.

If the trim is hardwood, predrilling the nail holes is a must. A good drill bit is a nail of the size being used to nail the trim. Cut the head off and sharpen the point.

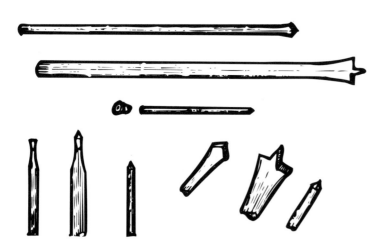

There should never be a shortage of drill bits of any size as long as there is a piece of stiff wire around. Big nails, little nails, welding rod—anything will do. Beat on the end to flatten and flair, then file cutting tips.

If you want a nail to slide into wood a little easier, rub it in your hair to pick up the oil.

Face oil works, too.

It acts like wax or soap on a wood screw.

Saliva on a wood screw will help if soap is not available.

When nailing thin brads, squeeze the brad with the fingers; it won't bend so easily.

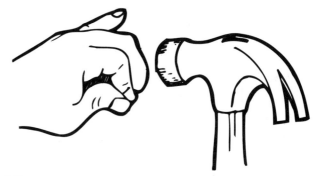

⏱ Fitting a Shelf

You can't just cut a board square at each end and expect it to fit in a corner. The joint compound buildup changes the angle in the corner, so it should be scribed.

The scribe tool is just a small compass that locks at any position desired.

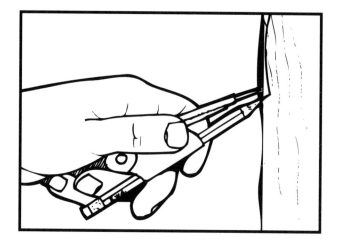

Set the scribe to the desired spacing and run the metal point along the wall. The pencil makes a parallel line.

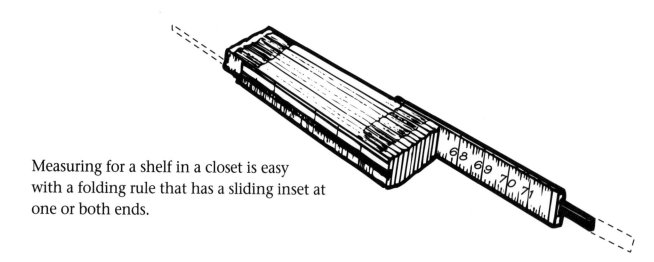

Measuring for a shelf in a closet is easy with a folding rule that has a sliding inset at one or both ends.

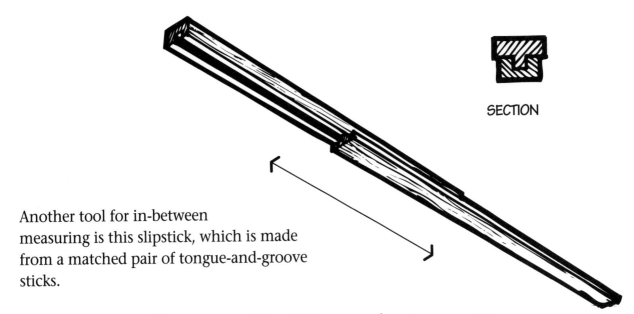

SECTION

Another tool for in-between measuring is this slipstick, which is made from a matched pair of tongue-and-groove sticks.

Both tools are used the same way. The rule has one advantage; you can read a number, and, if it slips, it can be reset to that number. The rule, though, unlike the slipstick, is limited to six feet.

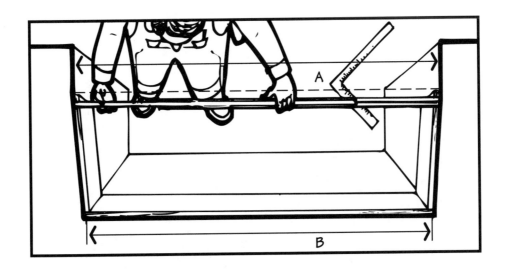

Use the folding rule or slipstick to find the longest dimension.

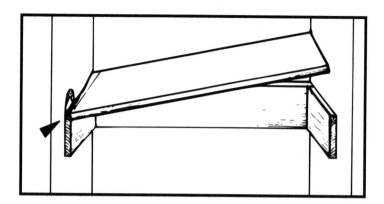

Cut the board a little longer than the longest dimension, put it in place tipped up at one end, and scribe. The scribe should be set to hit the corner of the edge, where there is space between the board and the wall.

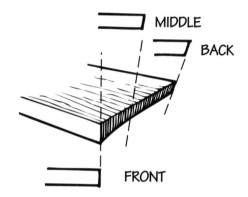

MIDDLE

BACK

FRONT

Cut this line, starting square at the front and back-cutting as you progress. Test this cut against the wall and correct with a block plane if necessary.

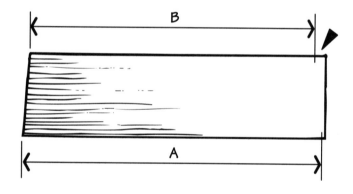

Measure the opening, front "A" and back "B," and transfer them to the shelf board.

Slip the shelf in place, tipped up at the other end, and scribe. The scribe should be set to hit one of the marks on the board and, when scribed, should hit the other mark. Cut this end the same way the other end was cut, and it should be a perfect fit. A little block planing might be in order. With the shelf in place, scribe and fit to the back wall.

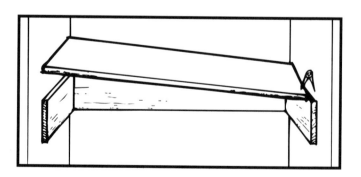

Although the frame work of stairs is not inside finish work, it ties in so closely that I have to include it here.

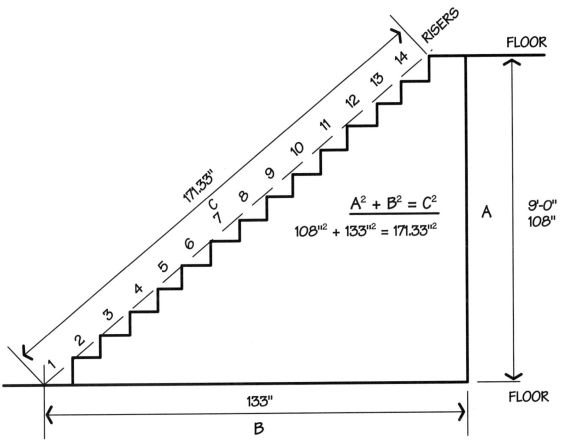

$$A^2 + B^2 = C^2$$
$$108^{\prime\prime 2} + 133^{\prime\prime 2} = 171.33^{\prime\prime 2}$$

The use of the calculator makes the mathematics of this job easy. To begin with, choose fourteen risers (about an average number), and divide that number into the floor-to-floor height (108 inches in this case). 108 inches divided by 14 = 7.71-inch riser.

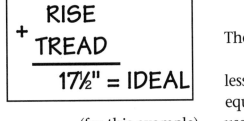

$$+\ \frac{\text{RISE}}{\text{TREAD}}{17\frac{1}{2}^{\prime\prime} = \text{IDEAL}}$$

(for this example)

The ideal rise plus tread total is 17½ inches
                    17.50" ideal total
less .... 7.71" the riser we came up with
equals .... 9.79" our ideal tread
- use .... 9.50" a stock tread size
times .... 14 tread spaces
equals .... 133"

From school, we remember $A^2+B^2=C^2$; so $108^2 + 133^2 = 171.3^2$

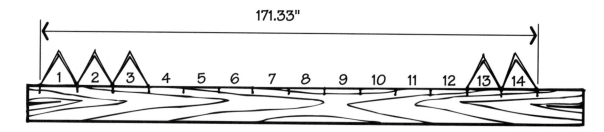

171.33"

Mark this dimension on a 15-foot 2x12. It will fit on a 14 footer, but the ends are usually split and may have other bad spots we would like to avoid. This 171.33 inches will have to be divided into the fourteen equal tread spaces with a pair of large dividers.

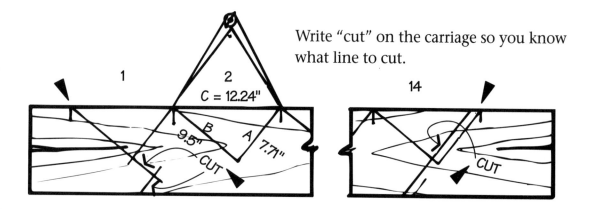

Write "cut" on the carriage so you know what line to cut.

The easiest way to find this spacing dimension is with the same $A^2+B^2=C^2$ formula.

$$A^2 + B^2 = C^2$$
$$7.71^{"2} + 9.5^{"2} = 12.24^{"2}$$

Set the dividers and walk them up the 2x12. With luck you will hit the 171.33-inch mark. Keep adjusting the dividers until you go from mark to mark fourteen times.

Mark the fourteen spaces clearly. Then set up a framing square with the rise and tread dimensions by clamping a 2x4 across it.

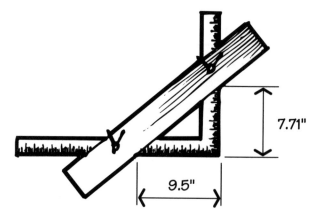

7.71"

9.5"

Start at either end and outline the rise and tread at each mark.

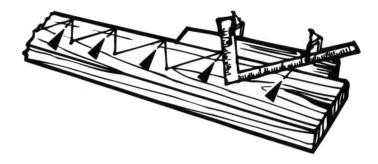

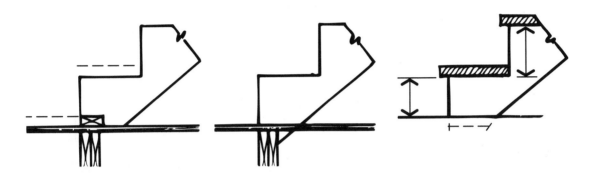

Mark the bottom of this carriage for whatever framing condition exists.

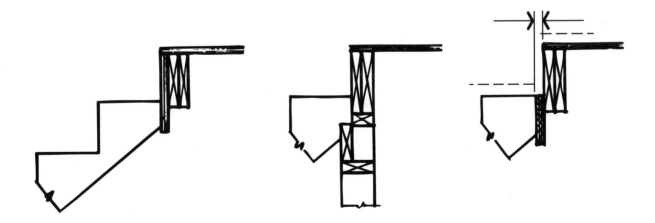

Mark the top of the carriage for the framing condition. Don't forget to take the finished floor into account on both top and bottom.

The carriage layout will look like this.

Double-check the layout before cutting. When satisfied, cut freehand with a power saw or handsaw. Run the cuts a little past where they intersect so that the triangles will fall out. We can use these later.

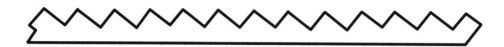

Now the carriage looks like this.

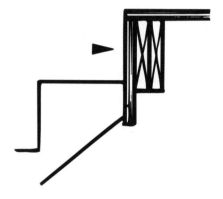

Try it in place and don't forget the ¾-inch hanger board if one is to be used.

Three carriages are usually required, so use the completed carriage as a pattern for the other 2x12s. A 2x6 with the triangular cutout blocks nailed on can be used for the middle carriage.

The middle carriage with blocks will look like this.

If a hanger board is used, nail the carriages to it and then nail the whole business in place.

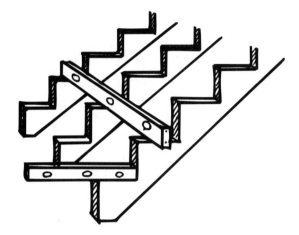

If all is well, the treads will be level.

For let-in treads with no risers, the basic layout is the same.

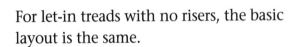

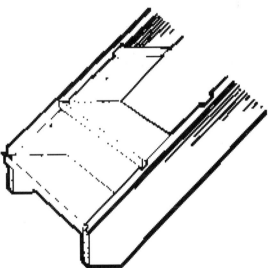

The grooves for the trades (usually 2x10) are made with a series of parallel cuts with a power saw set to the proper depth. Break away the pieces in the groove and clean up with a chisel.

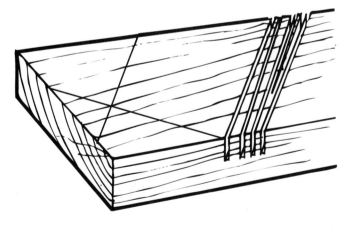

Here is the finished product.

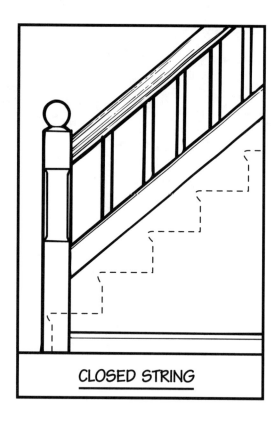

CLOSED STRING

2'-6" TO 2'-8"

OPEN STRING

Finishing a stairway is a measure-twice-cut-once, precision piece of carpentry. The first house I built has my first stairway, so it is not impossible even for a beginner. There are two types of stairways: the closed string and the open string.

This is an open string or stringer, mitered to receive the riser.

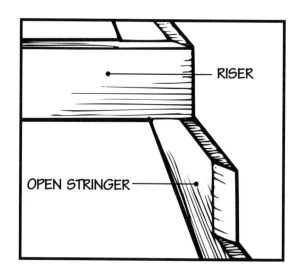

RISER

OPEN STRINGER

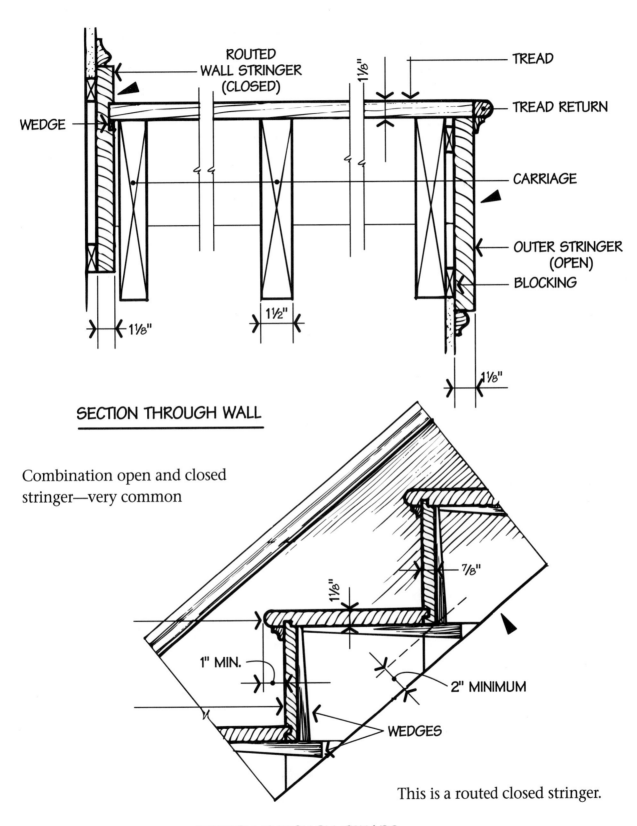

ROUTED
WALL STRINGER
(CLOSED)

1⅛"

TREAD

TREAD RETURN

WEDGE

CARRIAGE

OUTER STRINGER
(OPEN)

BLOCKING

1⅛"

1½"

1⅛"

SECTION THROUGH WALL

Combination open and closed
stringer—very common

7⁄8"

1⅛"

1" MIN.

2" MINIMUM

WEDGES

This is a routed closed stringer.

SECTION THROUGH TREADS

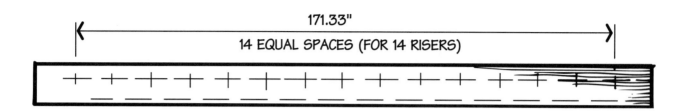

171.33"

14 EQUAL SPACES (FOR 14 RISERS)

The routed closed stringer is usually ¾-inch stock and is laid out the same way the carriage is laid out: by determining the number of risers and the length of tread and riser.

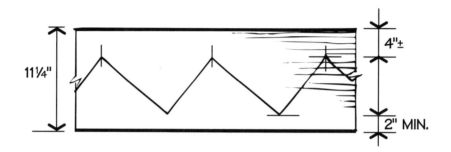

11¼"

4"±

2" MIN.

When the layout is made, leave at least a 2-inch clearance from the bottom of the stringer to the bottom junction where tread and riser meet. There should also be about 4 inches from the tread nosing to the top of the stringer. The total width of the stringer will be about 11¼ inches plus or minus.

Set up the framing square again, but this time allow for the 2-inch offset.

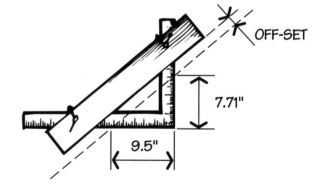

OFF-SET

7.71"

9.5"

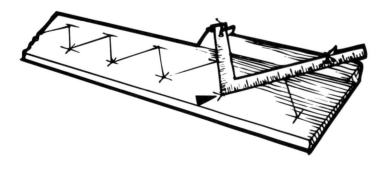

Hit the marks with the framing square.

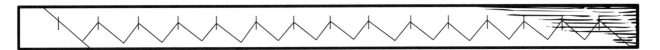

The riser and tread layout will look like this.

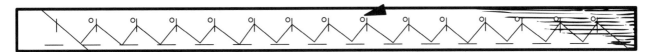

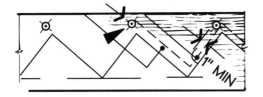

Locate and drill 1⅛-inch nosing holes for 1⅛-inch treads so that there will be a minimum 1-inch nosing overhang past the face of the riser. This plywood guide will work with a knife or router. One edge of the guide is for the top of the tread, and the other is for the bottom of the wedge. Clamp in place and do your stuff.

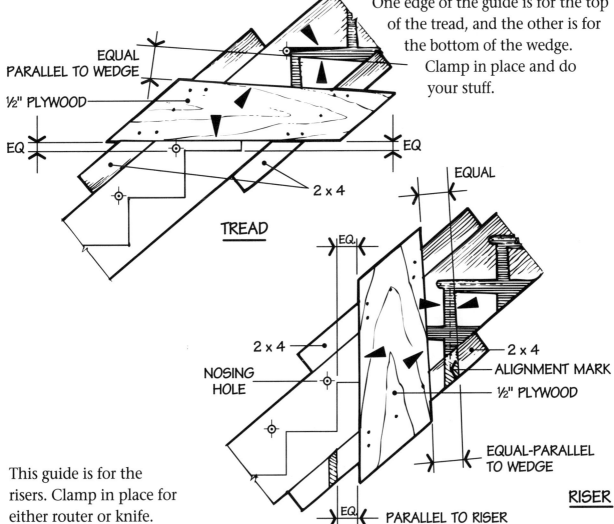

EQUAL
PARALLEL TO WEDGE

½" PLYWOOD

EQ   EQ

2 x 4

TREAD

EQUAL

EQ

2 x 4

NOSING
HOLE

2 x 4
ALIGNMENT MARK
½" PLYWOOD

EQUAL-PARALLEL
TO WEDGE

EQ   PARALLEL TO RISER

RISER

This guide is for the risers. Clamp in place for either router or knife.

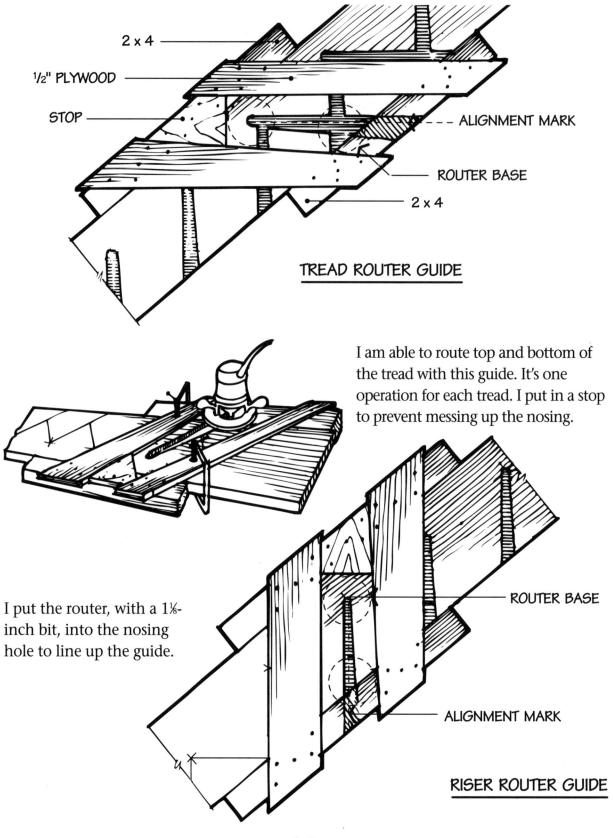

2 x 4

½" PLYWOOD

STOP

ALIGNMENT MARK

ROUTER BASE

2 x 4

TREAD ROUTER GUIDE

I am able to route top and bottom of the tread with this guide. It's one operation for each tread. I put in a stop to prevent messing up the nosing.

I put the router, with a 1⅛-inch bit, into the nosing hole to line up the guide.

ROUTER BASE

ALIGNMENT MARK

RISER ROUTER GUIDE

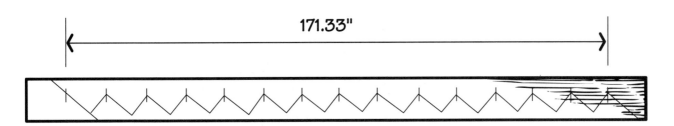

171.33"

The mitered open stringer is laid out the same way to start.

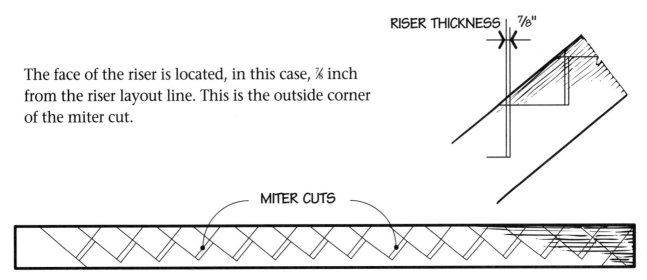

RISER THICKNESS | 7/8"

The face of the riser is located, in this case, ⅞ inch from the riser layout line. This is the outside corner of the miter cut.

MITER CUTS

The stringer is all laid out and ready to be cut with a power saw and guide or a handsaw. I prefer the handsaw.

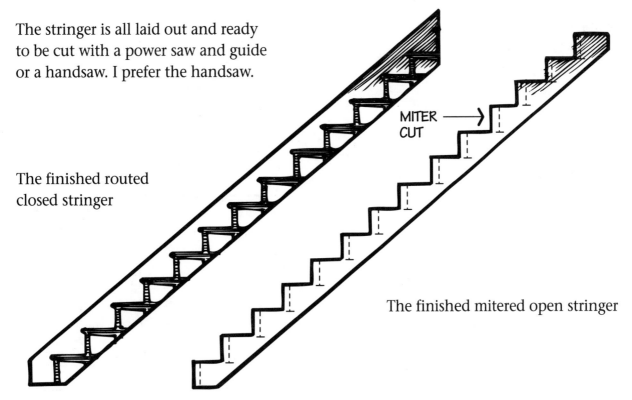

MITER CUT

The finished routed closed stringer

The finished mitered open stringer

Risers and treads
stocked at lumber
yards are either
shiplapped and
grooved . . .

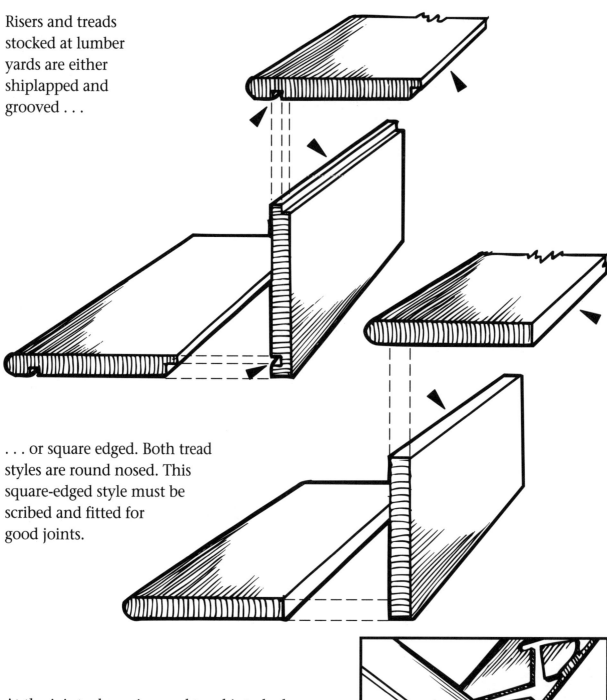

. . . or square edged. Both tread
styles are round nosed. This
square-edged style must be
scribed and fitted for
good joints.

At the joint where riser and tread interlock
(front and back), wedges and blocks are glued as
you progress. The wedges are driven in to force
the face of the tread and riser against the face of
the routed stringer. Don't spare the glue.

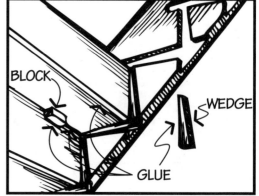

BLOCK

WEDGE

GLUE

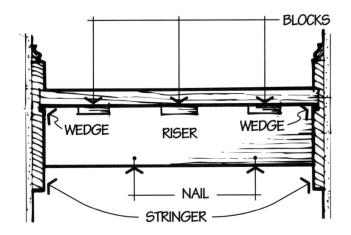

The routed closed-stringer stairway does not have carriages because it is assembled from the underside. Start at the top, installing the tread first.

The scribed-and-butted closed stringer does have carriages, and it is assembled from the topside, starting from the top and putting in the tread first.

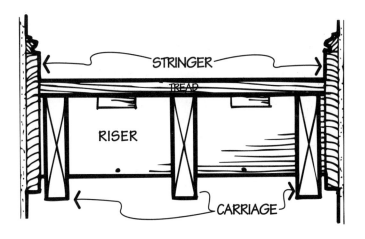

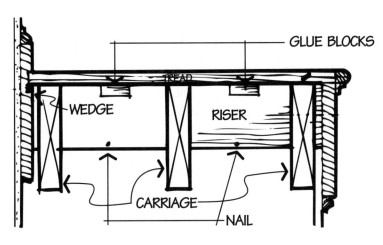

The combination open-and-closed stringer uses carriages and is assembled from the topside, starting from the bottom and putting in the risers first.

Nailing hardwood flooring is greatly eased with the use of the nailing machine. These machines can be rented.

The old flooring hammer will also do the trick. This hammer weighs about 25 ounces and has a little bigger head and a longer handle. The head is also a harder steel than a standard hammer to handle the hard flooring nails.

No matter what tool you use, the bent-over position is the one assumed for the whole job.

It's best to have the flooring stock on the job a few days in the heated house, preferably unbundled, so that the strips can adjust to the climate.

The strips are best laid running the long way in the room.

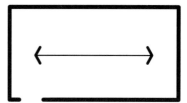

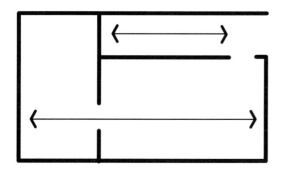

When a room opens to another room or hall, keep the strips running in the same direction.

The strips can go either way with diagonal subflooring, but the strongest condition is to run the strips perpendicular to the joists. With diagonal subflooring, this is always possible.

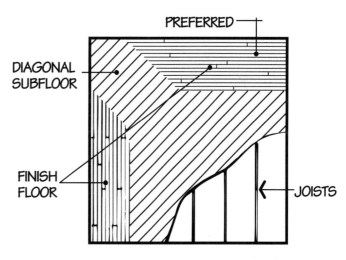

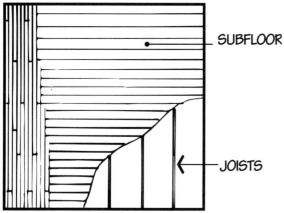

With the subfloor running perpendicular to the joists, the finished floor should run perpendicular to the subfloor for the strongest condition.

⊟ Hardwood Flooring

With plywood subflooring, the strongest condition is with the strips running perpendicular to the joists, but either way is OK.

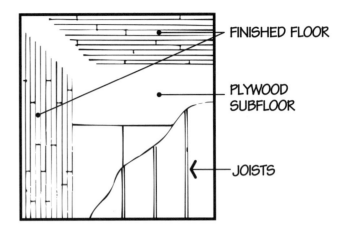

FINISHED FLOOR

PLYWOOD SUBFLOOR

JOISTS

The first thing to do before starting the flooring is a clean sweep.

Then roll out 15# building paper on the floor being laid. Lap the edges a few inches to keep dust, dirt, and dampness from the flooring.

To establish the location of the first strip of flooring, snap a chalk line or stretch a string 6 or 8 inches from the wall and parallel. The string is better because the paper is liable to move, changing the chalk-line location. Start the first strip ½ inch from the wall and keep it parallel to the string or chalk line.

CHALK LINE

STRING

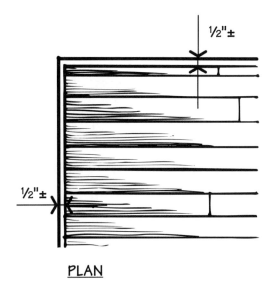

1/2"±

1/2"±

PLAN

The flooring is kept about ½ inch away from the wall all around to allow the flooring to expand.

The base or shoe base covers this space.

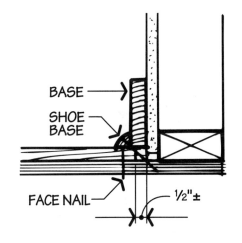

BASE

SHOE
BASE

FACE NAIL

1/2"±

6" TO 8"

Face-nail this first piece using a cutoff finish nail to predrill. Lay out a few rows ahead so you just have to move the strips into place and nail them home. Stagger the joints 6 to 8 inches.

The skill required with the hammer is not necessary with the nailing machine.

This is the basic working position for hammer and machine.

The nailing is done between the feet.

Drive the nail almost home, just short of hitting the flooring with the hammer.

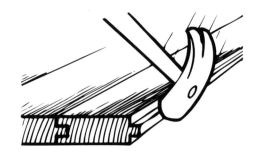

Lay a round nail set on the head and drive it home with the hammer, being careful not to hit the flooring.

The machine, loaded with nails, is placed over the edge of the flooring and pounded with a heavy mallet. It's the way to go.

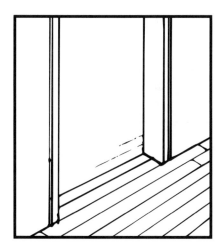

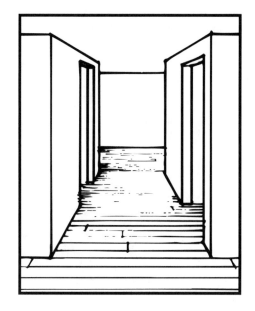

Mix short pieces with long ones; but in halls and doorways where there is a lot a traffic, use long pieces. Use extra short and bad-looking pieces in closets.

Stand on both the strip going in and the previous one to align and to hold it in place.

Use a block of flooring material to take the hammer blows if a piece of flooring is tough to get in tightly. The nailing machine acts the same way when it's pounded with the heavy mallet.

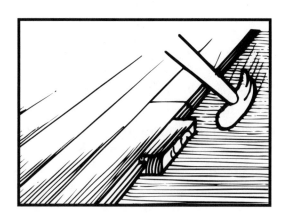

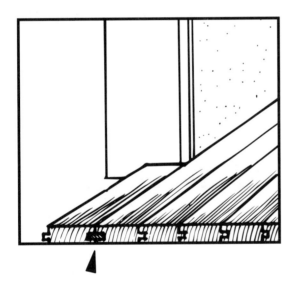

When working from a wall alongside a closet, lay the floor up to the closet face and reverse the flooring going into the closet. When you reverse, the strips will be groove to groove. A spline cut to fit will take care of that. The rest of the flooring goes in one direction, while the closet flooring goes in the other.

The last piece of flooring is ripped, drilled, and wedged into position with a pry bar before nailing. Be sure to protect the wall or baseboard with a block of wood.

An old-time cabinet maker told me always to use plywood ledger strips for supporting countertops because they won't shrink.

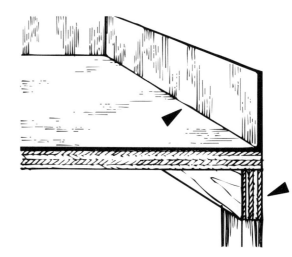

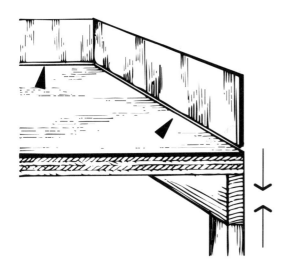

Solid stock will shrink, causing a gap between the backsplash and the countertop.

All plywood seams should be well blocked underneath.

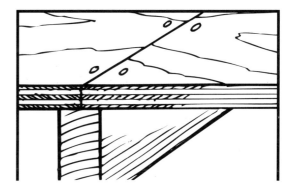

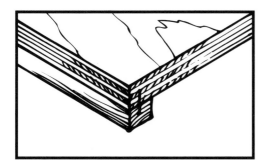

I like this kind of nosing; the top is more solid.

Nosing applied to the face of the countertop can loosen, disturbing a Formica corner.

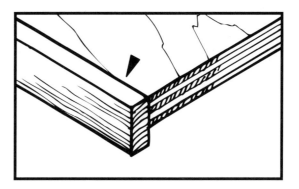

Fill all seams and depressions; set and fill all nail holes; finally, sand the whole business.

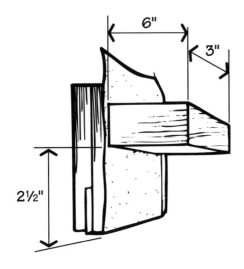

Make up a simple jig from scrap wood to sand the edges.

I have put in many plastic-laminate countertops using a saw, chisel, block plane, and a file, but I now have a few simple tools to make the job easier. The quality doesn't change with these tools, but the speed does.

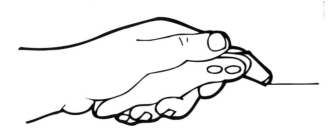

The simplest tool for cutting plastic laminate is a knife with a carbide tip.

Put a straightedge on the plastic-laminate sheet and score with the knife. It might take a few strokes. Then snap along the scored line. Put the straight-edge on the good side of the line. If the knife runs off the line, the good piece won't be ruined. You can even cut holes for switches and sinks with this tool. It

has to be used with care because it doesn't control too easily (it is difficult to start and stop the cuts). A few practice cuts will help your confidence.

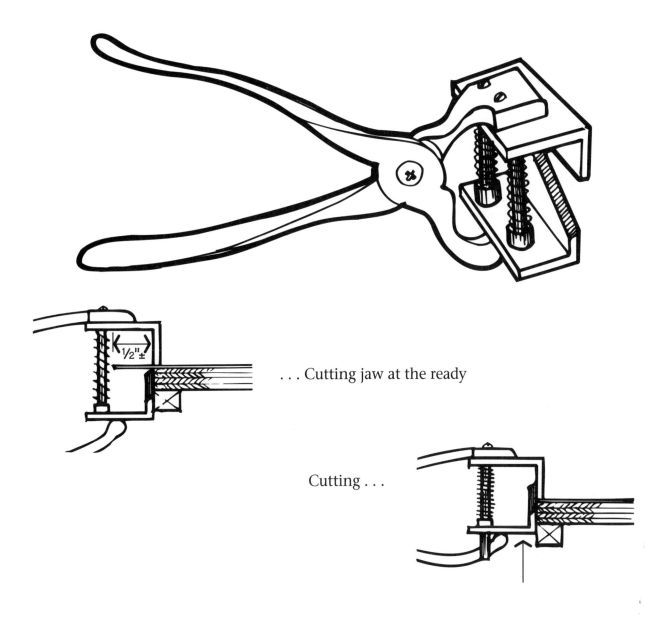

. . . Cutting jaw at the ready

Cutting . . .

Another great tool is this pair of shears. After plastic laminate is installed, these shears will cut right to the edge with a clean cut. The sheet should have no more than a ½-inch overhang. This tool also cuts right up to the wall, unlike a router, which leaves a few inches to chisel. The knife cuts the sheets to the approximate size, and then the shears trim them to the exact size after they are cemented in place. A file is used to ease the sharp corner. Someone permanently borrowed my shears, and I have not been able to find a replacement. There are hand-held shears that look and cut like tin snips.

The edging is put on before the top. 1½-inch edging pieces are available, or they can be cut with a knife or on the table saw using a plywood-cutting blade.

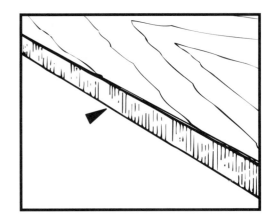

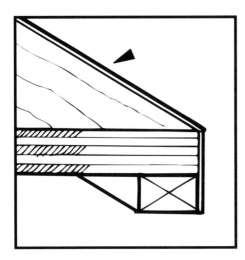

It can easily be put on flush with the top. Put a good edge up for a tight corner.

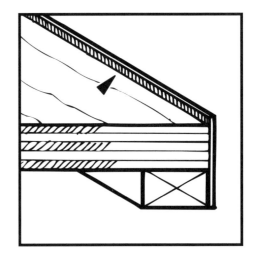

It can be put on with a little overhang and trimmed with a router or my special shears, which I no longer have.

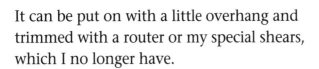

ABOUT HALF
THIS WILL DO

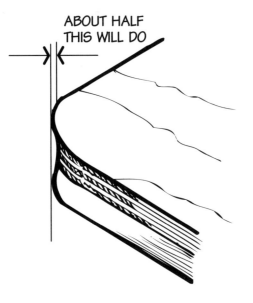

Rounded corners are easy if a little care is taken when cutting the plywood top. I like to concave the face a little to be sure the top and bottom of the Formica edging have good contact. When this edging is bent, the face will be slightly concave.

The edge must also be square with the top.

This jig will help.

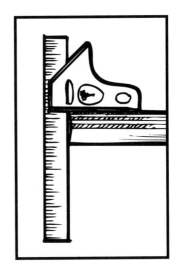

Plastic laminate will follow large curves with no trouble, but small curves need help. Heat is the help needed, and a hot plate or stove will do the job. First, test a sample piece of edging by resting it a few inches from the heat and timing how long it takes to "pop." Now take a good piece, heat it just short of that time . . .

and bend it around the curve. There should be no cement on the edging or the counter face. You are just preforming the edging. Remember, too, that some contact cement is flammable, so be careful. The preformed edge can then be cemented in place. Another way is to thin the strip on the back side, where the curve is to be, with a block plane. This system has limitations.

A file laid flat on the countertop and run along the edge will take care of any high spots the edging might have.

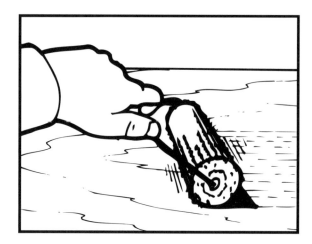

The easiest and quickest way to apply contact cement is with a paint roller.

The fumes will make you light-headed in a hurry, so ventilate the area or wear a protective fume respirator.

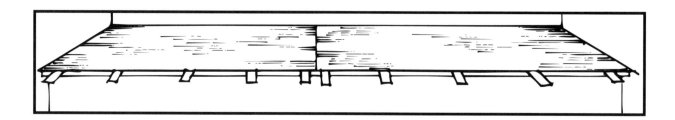

On a long counter, and when more than one piece of plastic laminate is to be put down, ¼-inch strips of wood about 12 inches apart will keep the cement-coated sheets off the cement-coated plywood so that they can be positioned. Venetian-blind strips, the curved aluminum kind, work even better. They slide out easier.

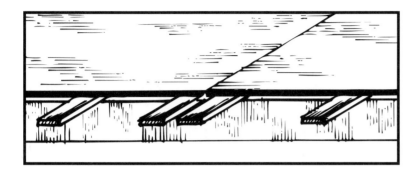

Put a strip on each side of the seam.

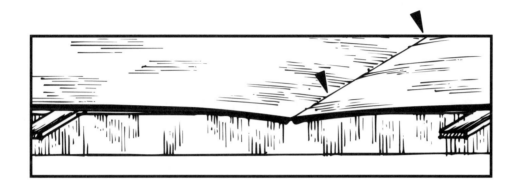

Pull the straps at the seam first, making sure the seam is perfect. Then pull the strips farthest away and work toward the seam. This will drive the two sheets together, making a tight fit at the seam.

The safest way to cement an odd-shaped backsplash that tucks up under cabinets is with wallboard mastic. It allows you to move the sheet around on the wall. Contact cement is good if there are enough hands to hold the sheet off the wall while it is being positioned.

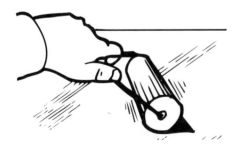

Once the sheets are cemented in place, they should be rolled with a 6-inch hard-rubber roller to get the air out and make a good bond.

A block of wood and a hammer work, too. Be sure to go over the whole surface.

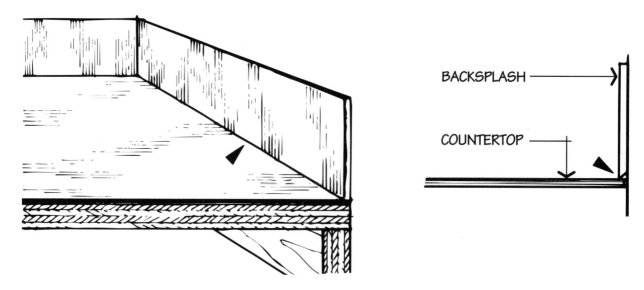

BACKSPLASH

COUNTERTOP

Countertops go on before the backsplash, and, like closet shelves, the edges that run along the walls have to be scribed. It doesn't have to be a super fit because the backsplash will cover any imperfections. The backsplash does have to be a good scribe fit.

A good tool for this is a sharp block plane. Like any good butt joint, plane it so that the face edge is strong. As long as the plane is sharp, it works similar to planing wood; but when it dulls (and it dulls quickly), the work gets difficult. The procedure to follow: scribe, plane, fit (almost), scribe, plane, fit (you hope).

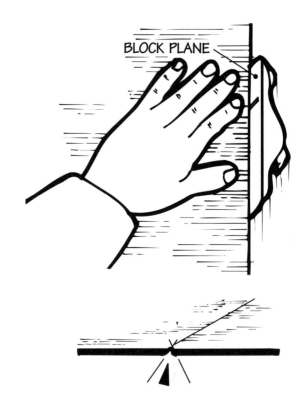

BLOCK PLANE

To plane plastic laminate, hold the sheet, with just a little overhang, at the edge of the counter. Hold the sheet down with one hand while making clean, sure strokes with the plane. Try longish strokes rather than short choppy ones. Keep the plane sharp.

When butting pieces, use the same back-cutting technique to ensure a tight fit on top.

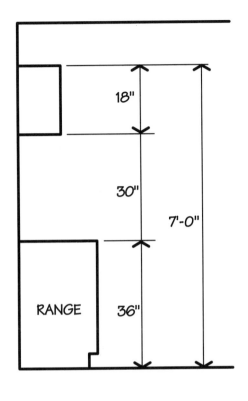

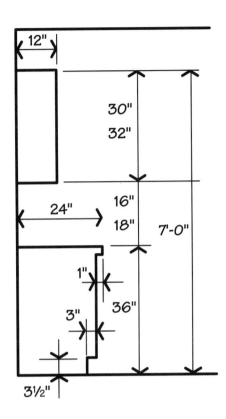

If kitchen cabinets are to be homemade (custom), any size will do; but there are some basic, standard dimensions.

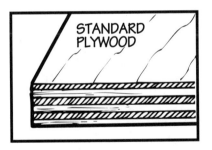

Another consideration is the material. Again, anything will do, but the best choice in plywood is lumber core. It's expensive, so use only where necessary. It's made up of three layers: a veneer on each side of solid strips of wood.

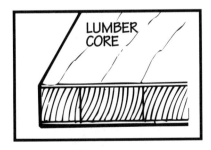

The edges can be covered with solid strips, or a triangular piece can be glued in.

Use the rabbet joint whenever possible. It's strong and neat.

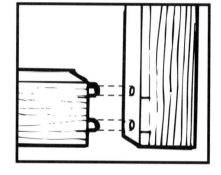

Doweled joints can't be beat.

These are minimum lengths. Use longer screws when work permits and predrill. Glue joints where possible. Drywall or drywall-type screws are best, and the best tool for driving them in is a cordless driver-drill.

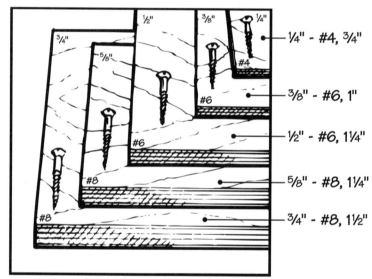

- ¼" - #4, ¾"
- ⅜" - #6, 1"
- ½" - #6, 1¼"
- ⅝" - #8, 1¼"
- ¾" - #8, 1½"

Predrill if nailing is close to the edge.

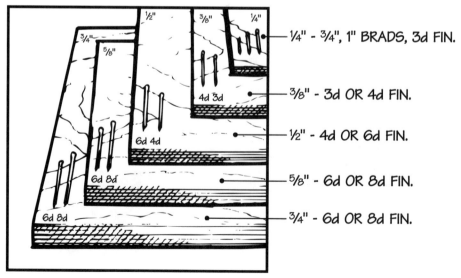

- ¼" - ¾", 1" BRADS, 3d FIN.
- ⅜" - 3d OR 4d FIN.
- ½" - 4d OR 6d FIN.
- ⅝" - 6d OR 8d FIN.
- ¾" - 6d OR 8d FIN.

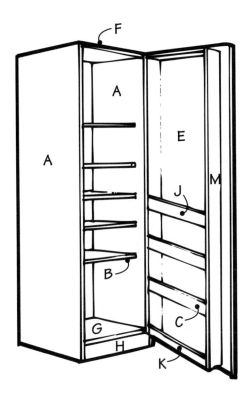

Before starting construction on cabinets, there should be a drawing of some sort that all the parts can be letter coded on.

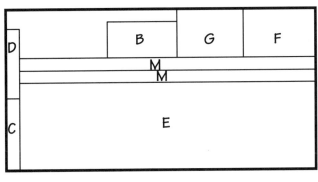

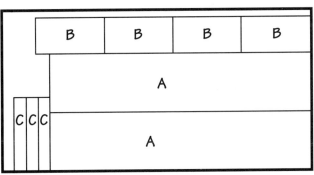

Then, on graph paper, lay out a 4x8 plywood shape (about 1 inch equals 12 inches) and fit the parts in. Keep the grain direction and saw-cut width in mind. The number of sheets required for the job is easy to figure from these layouts. They don't have to be fancy.

The depth of the base is controlled by the cabinet front frame.

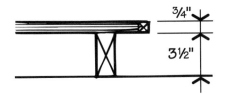

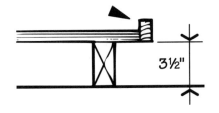

. . . This condition is hard to clean.

This is fairly common.

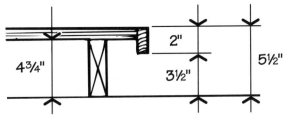

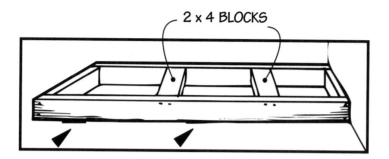

2 x 4 BLOCKS

There are many ways to build cabinets, and I like to build base cabinets on a leveled 1½- x 4¾-inch base. Level up with wood-shingle tips. The base is designed so that the interior partitions can be centered on 2x4 blocks built into the base.

Pencil the cabinet outline on the wall. Screw the ¾-inch plywood counter support ¾ inch down from the level countertop line. Be sure to find the studs with the screws. Now it's ready to build on.

¾"   TOP OF COUNTER

Whether the cabinets are cut and fit as you go or precut, this system works nicely. I start with the wall piece that is notched to fit snugly under the wall rail piece (counter support). Keep this piece ¾ inch from the wall marks. The floor piece follows. If the base is level, all should go well.

Plumb the partitions as you go.

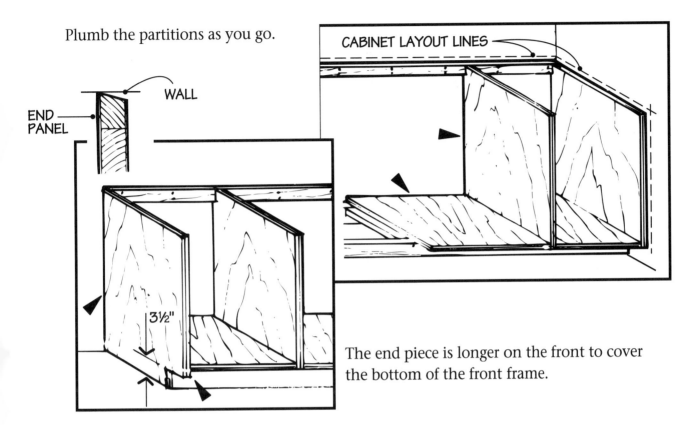

WALL

END PANEL

CABINET LAYOUT LINES

3½"

The end piece is longer on the front to cover the bottom of the front frame.

The frame can be prebuilt or cut and fit. If prebuilt, dowel and glue joints. If cut and fit, glue and nail joints.

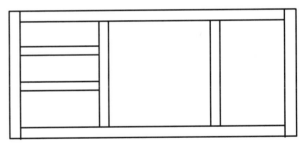

To allow for scribing, make the frame a tad wider and bevel the edge that hits the wall.

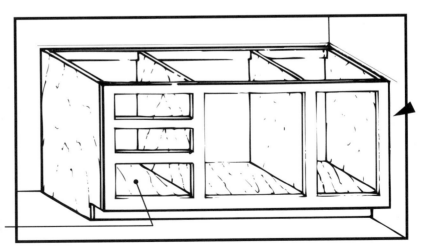

THIS PANEL IS NOT NECESSARY IF THERE IS A DRAWER HERE.

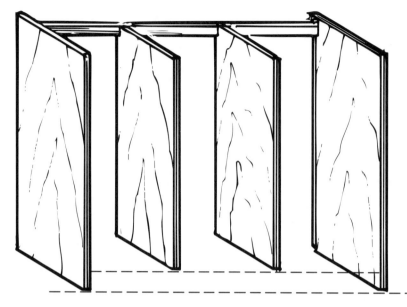

I build the upper cabinets with interior partitions like the base cabinets. Note that the middle partitions are shorter so that they can sit on top of the bottom piece.

The top and bottom are one-piece sections.

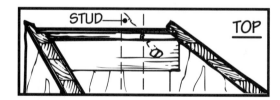

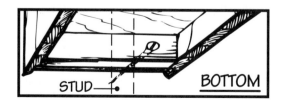

There are cleats at the top and bottom for fastening the cabinet to the wall.

If the cabinet starts at a wall, make the side rail wide and beveled to allow for scribing.

Here again, the front frame can be prebuilt or cut and fit as you go.

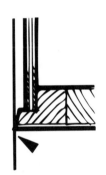

The side panels are rabbeted and beveled for scribing.

Doors can be square-edged or lipped.

DOOR   DOOR

A jig for locating door-pull holes will speed things up.

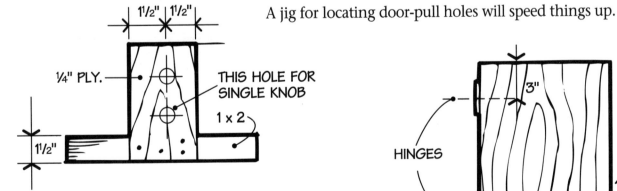

1½" 1½"

¼" PLY.

THIS HOLE FOR
SINGLE KNOB

1 x 2

1½"

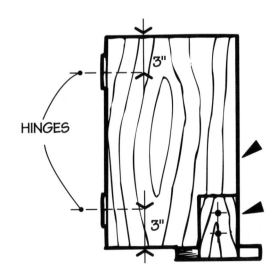

3"

HINGES

3"

Make it so that when held tight to the bottom or top and flush to the door edge, the holes will be right. It is both a left and a right jig.

To hang wall cabinets, a couple of wood helpers make the job easy. They should be a little short so that the cabinets can be shimmed to the right height.

When everything is lined up, check the fit at the wall. Scribe and plane if necessary.

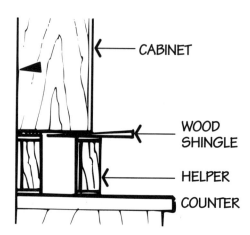

If all is well, find the studs, drill, and screw. It will take a 3-inch screw, so have some soap on hand. Driving in 3-inch deck screws with a driver-drill works best.

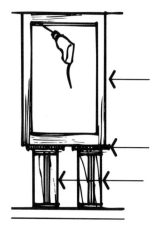

Drawers should be solid and easy to operate. The smoothest operating slides are store-bought, and there are many types. A simple system is to extend a ½-inch plywood bottom to the sides and run it in grooves in the side panels. Use plenty of paraffin or silicone to help the action.

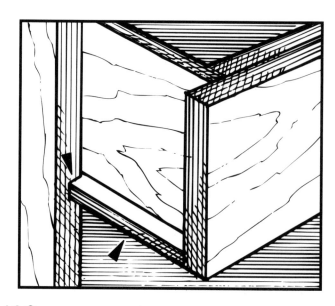

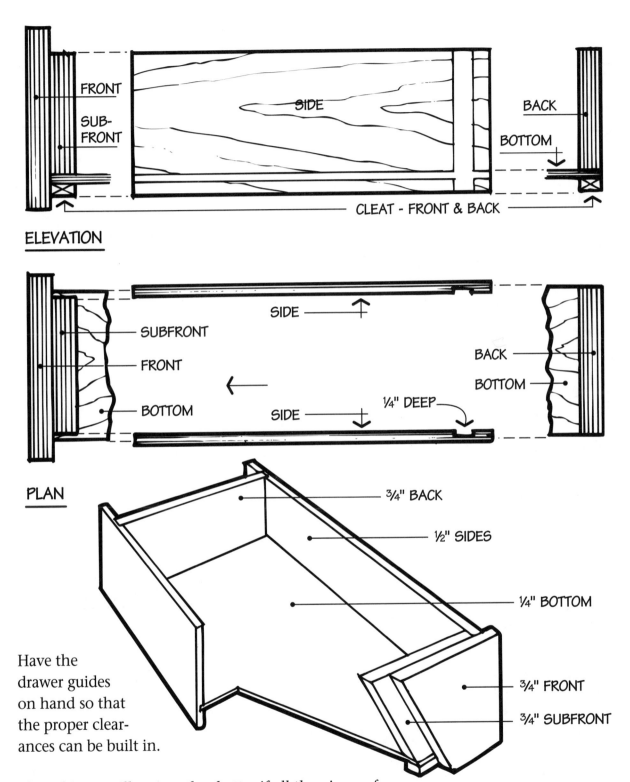

ELEVATION

FRONT
SUB-FRONT
SIDE
BACK
BOTTOM
CLEAT - FRONT & BACK

PLAN

SUBFRONT
FRONT
SIDE
BACK
BOTTOM
SIDE
BOTTOM
¼" DEEP

¾" BACK
½" SIDES
¼" BOTTOM
¾" FRONT
¾" SUBFRONT

Have the
drawer guides
on hand so that
the proper clear-
ances can be built in.

The cabinets will go together better if all the pieces of
the same dimension are cut with the same saw setting. In this case, the subbase and back
are the same height; the bottom and back are the same width.

SAP SIDE

HEART SIDE

A wide wood panel is almost impossible to keep from cupping on the sap side.

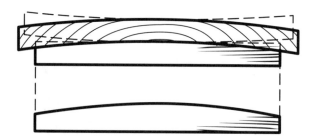

My dad overcame this by screwing curved cleats to the backside of the panel. They pull the panel to a curve opposite the original cup.

The board will try to cup again but will go just so far. How much to curve the cleats is pretty much guesswork. A piece of angle iron screwed to the back will also work.

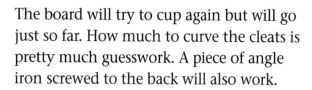

Nothing disturbs a room more than a sagging book shelf. Stock ¾ inch thick should be no longer than 30 inches.

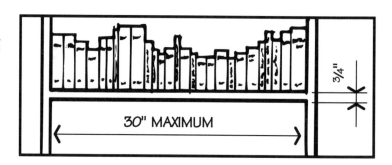

30" MAXIMUM

3/4"

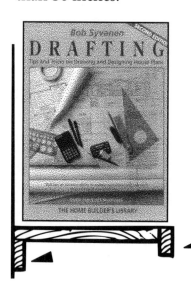

The longer the shelf, the thicker it should be unless it has support front and back.

Strong, neat shelves can be made with grooved side panels.

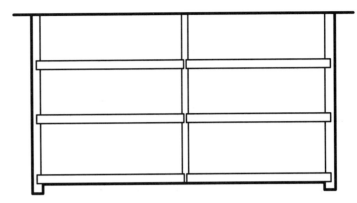

Lining up the adjacent groove is always a tough job.

This jig made of ¾-inch plywood makes easy work of it. Make the spacers thinner than the board being grooved or shim the board with a piece of cardboard to insure a good grip by the jig.

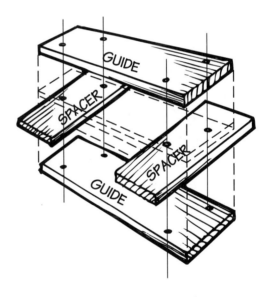

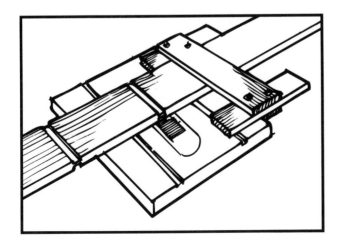

Use the edge of the table to run the guide against. Flip the whole business over and cut the matching groove. Make sure the jig is cutting square.

I like to set up a work table as soon as possible. Find a long, free space where a 14-foot 2x10 plank can be set up. A height of 37 inches suits me.

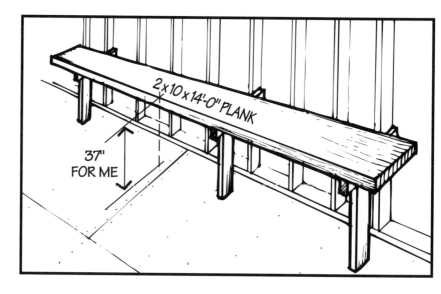

2x10x14'-0" PLANK

37" FOR ME

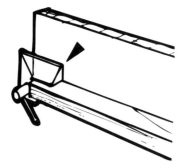

A carpenter's vise at one end is a great help.

When easing corners with a block plane, run the plane the length of the board in one stroke. This will give a nice, even chamfer.

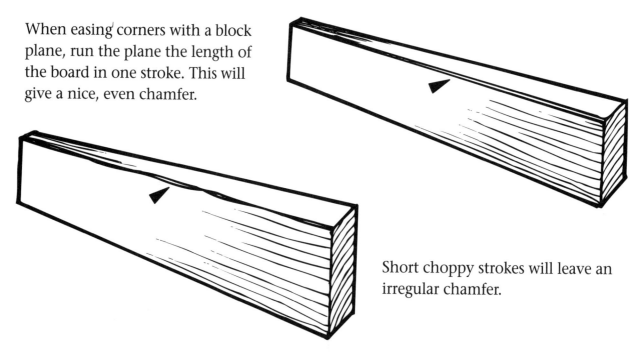

Short choppy strokes will leave an irregular chamfer.

The same applies for any planing: Long, smooth strokes make for a smooth job. Keep the area along the work table clear so that there is no stopping as you walk with the plane from end to end.

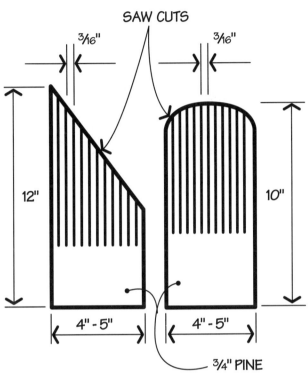

SAW CUTS

3/16"   3/16"

12"   10"

4" - 5"   4" - 5"

3/4" PINE

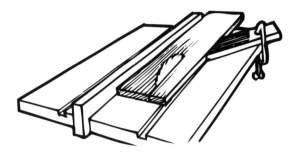

Spring blocks clamped to the table-saw top keep stock being ripped against the rip fence while you concentrate on pushing the piece through.

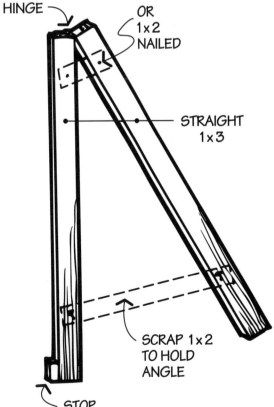

HINGE

OR
1x2
NAILED

STRAIGHT
1x3

SCRAP 1x2
TO HOLD
ANGLE

STOP

A quickie taper jig can be made with two 1x3x20- or 24-inch pieces of straight stock, with a hinge or 1x2 block at one end and a 1x2 tacked at the other to hold the angle. Add a stop at the bottom of one leg, and it's ready to go.

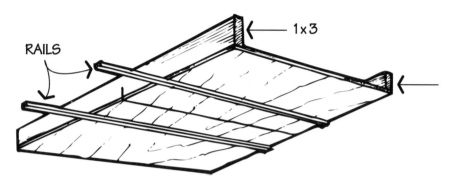

RAILS

1 x 3

This is a handy jig for cutting wide boards and is nice for cabinet work. Spray the rails with silicone for easy sliding.

This is a nice jig for making raised panels on the table saw. Spray the rip fence for easy sliding.

14"

5"

3"

15"

TO FIT TABLE
SAW RIP FENCE

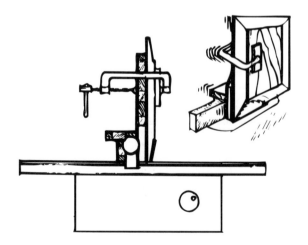

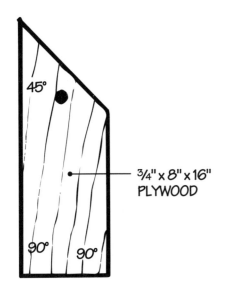

3/4" x 8" x 16"
PLYWOOD

45°

90°   90°

The miter gauge on a table saw can be quickly checked if a pattern is kept handy.

Sharpening stones should be kept in a box and wiped clean after every sharpening. A quick way to make a box is to put the stone on a piece of ¾-inch pine (larger than the stone) and nail some strips, one-half the thickness (plus a tad) of the stone on the board, all around the stone. Make two like this and trim to size on the table saw. Keep a little clearance between the strips and the stone.

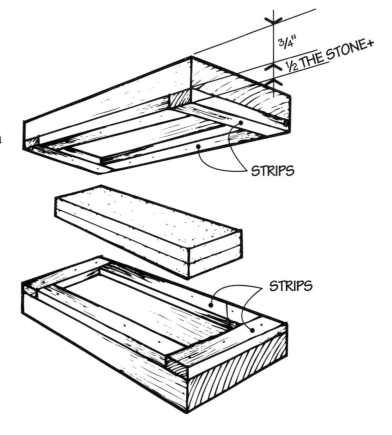

3/4"
½ THE STONE+

STRIPS

STRIPS

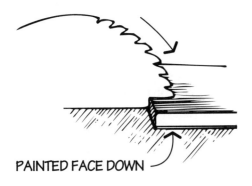

PAINTED FACE DOWN

When cutting wood painted on one side, put the painted side down so the blade won't dull as quickly.

Gluing pieces of wood together sounds simple, but there are some basic techniques that can help.

When gluing boards edge to edge for a bench or tabletop, the sap and heart faces should alternate to maintain a flat surface.

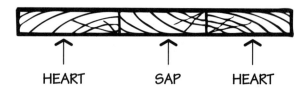

HEART   SAP   HEART

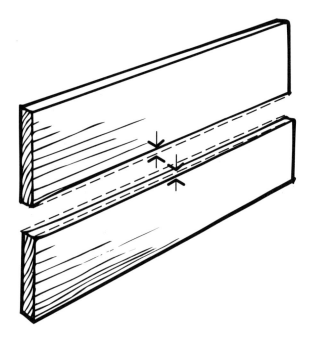

They should be planed, slightly, at the center, tapering to no planing at the ends. The edge of the boards will shrink more than the middle, so everything will equalize. If this planing isn't done, the ends will shrink and split. Observe how boards split at the ends.

Two boards glued face-to-face should have the sap faces together and the grain running in the same direction, not crossgrained like plywood.

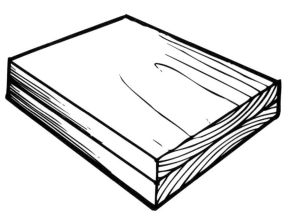

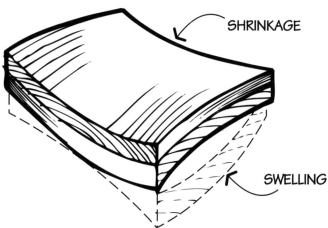

SHRINKAGE

SWELLING

If two boards are cross-grained, the chances for warping are great. Three boards can be cross-grained.

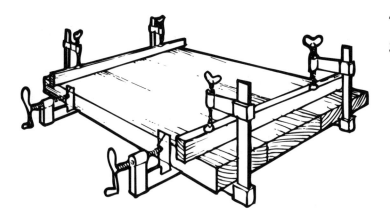

This is the best way to clamp edge-glued boards.

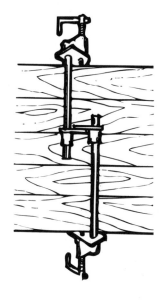

If bar clamps are too short, they can be used in combination.

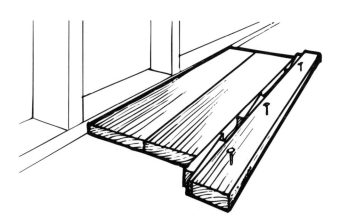

Here is a quickie way to edge-glue boards. Some weights on the top will keep the boards from buckling.

Miters are tough to clamp, but two blocks tacked on the outside will make clamping possible.

If there is water available, this is a good way to get some pressure for face gluing.

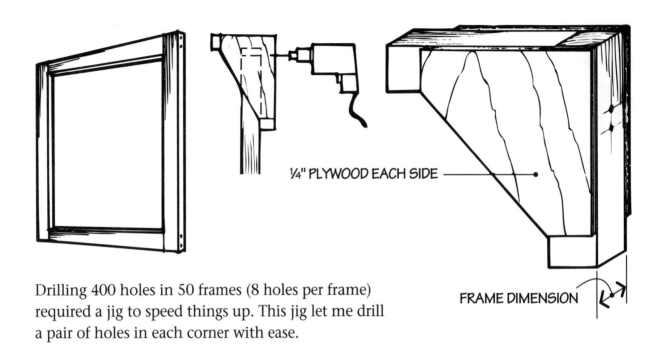

¼" PLYWOOD EACH SIDE

FRAME DIMENSION

Drilling 400 holes in 50 frames (8 holes per frame) required a jig to speed things up. This jig let me drill a pair of holes in each corner with ease.

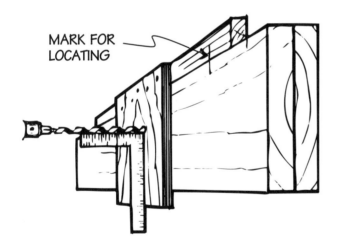

MARK FOR LOCATING

Twenty-two beams 20 inches thick had to be drilled from each side and the holes had to meet. I made a jig to line up the drilling, and it worked great.

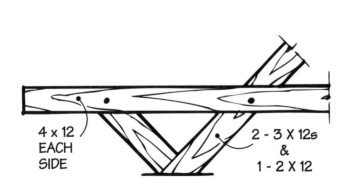

4 x 12 EACH SIDE

2 - 3 X 12s & 1 - 2 X 12

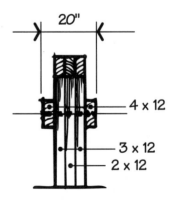

20"

4 x 12

3 x 12

2 x 12

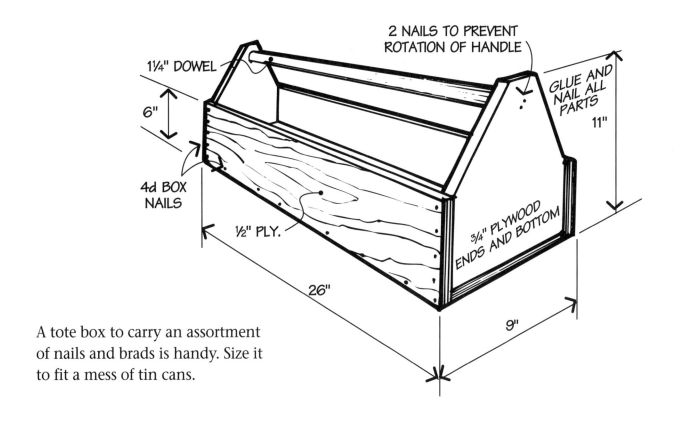

1¼" DOWEL

2 NAILS TO PREVENT
ROTATION OF HANDLE

GLUE AND NAIL ALL PARTS

6"

11"

4d BOX NAILS

½" PLY.

¾" PLYWOOD ENDS AND BOTTOM

26"

9"

A tote box to carry an assortment
of nails and brads is handy. Size it
to fit a mess of tin cans.

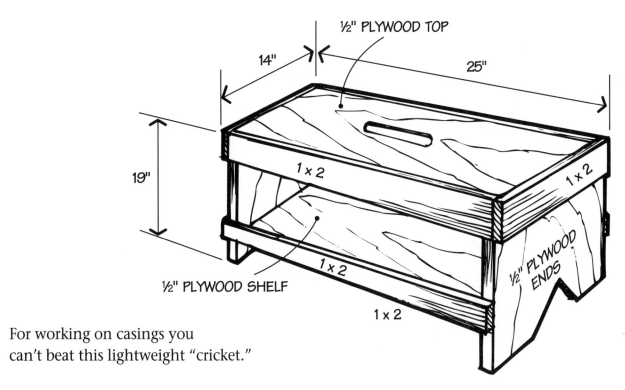

½" PLYWOOD TOP

14"

25"

19"

1 x 2

1 x 2

1 x 2

½" PLYWOOD ENDS

½" PLYWOOD SHELF

1 x 2

For working on casings you
can't beat this lightweight "cricket."

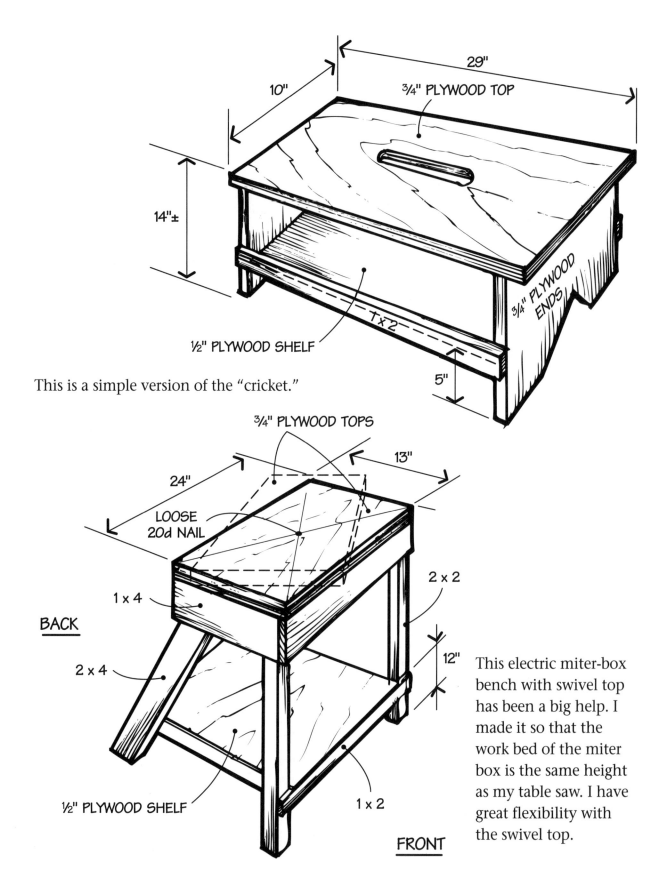

29"

10"

¾" PLYWOOD TOP

14"±

½" PLYWOOD SHELF

1 x 2

¾" PLYWOOD ENDS

5"

This is a simple version of the "cricket."

¾" PLYWOOD TOPS

24"

13"

LOOSE 20d NAIL

BACK

1 x 4

2 x 2

2 x 4

12"

½" PLYWOOD SHELF

1 x 2

FRONT

This electric miter-box bench with swivel top has been a big help. I made it so that the work bed of the miter box is the same height as my table saw. I have great flexibility with the swivel top.

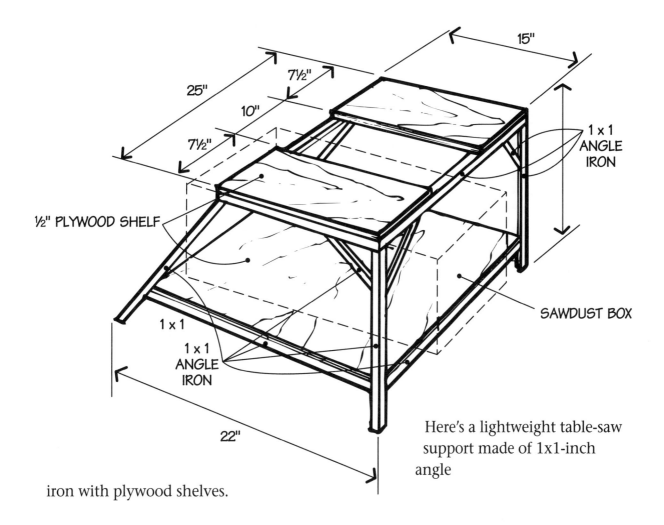

15"

25"

7½"

10"

7½"

1 x 1
ANGLE
IRON

½" PLYWOOD SHELF

SAWDUST BOX

1 x 1

1 x 1
ANGLE
IRON

22"

Here's a lightweight table-saw support made of 1x1-inch angle

iron with plywood shelves.

A sawdust box under the table saw keeps the area clean; but when the arbor nut falls into the sawdust, it is almost impossible to find. Keep a magnet handy, and fishing out metal in the sawdust box will be a snap.

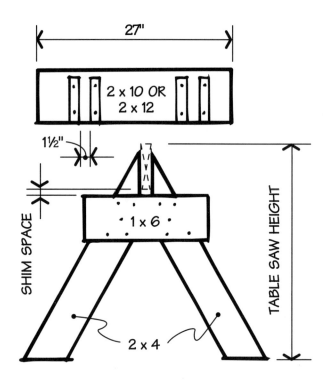

27'

2 x 10 OR
2 x 12

1½"

SHIM SPACE

1 x 6

2 x 4

TABLE SAW HEIGHT

This is a quickie work support for the table saw. It comes apart, is easily stored, and adjusts for height.

37"±

I made the height of all my equipment the same so that I could use the pieces with each other.